THE SERVICE STATE

Rhetoric, Reality and Promise

Governance Series

Governance is the process of effective coordination whereby an organization or a system guides itself when resources, power, and information are widely distributed. Studying governance means probing the pattern of rights and obligations that underpins organizations and social systems, understanding how they coordinate their parallel activities and maintain their coherence, exploring the sources of dysfunction, and suggesting ways to redesign organizations whose governance is in need of repair.

The series welcomes a range of contributions—from conceptual and theoretical reflections, ethnographic and case studies, and proceedings of conferences and symposia, to works of a very practical nature—that deal with problems or issues on the governance front. The series publishes works both in French and in English.

The Governance Series is part of the publications division of the Centre on Governance at the University of Ottawa. This is the 25th volume published in the series. The Centre on Governance also publishes a quarterly electronic journal, www.optimumonline.ca.

The published titles in the series are listed at the end of this book.

THE SERVICE STATE

Rhetoric, Reality and Promise

Patrice Dutil, Cosmo Howard,
John Langford and Jeffrey Roy

UNIVERSITY OF OTTAWA PRESS
OTTAWA

University of Ottawa Press
542 King Edward Avenue
Ottawa, ON K1N 6N5
www.press.uottawa.ca

uOttawa

The University of Ottawa Press acknowledges with gratitude the support extended to its publishing list by Heritage Canada through its Book Publishing Industry Development Program,
by the Canada Council for the Arts, by the Canadian Federation for the Humanities and
Social Sciences through its Aid to Scholarly Publications Program, by the Social Sciences
and Humanities Research Council, and by the University of Ottawa.

LIBRARY AND ARCHIVES CANADA CATALOGUING IN PUBLICATION

The service state : rhetoric, reality and promise / Patrice Dutil ... [et al.].

(Governance series, ISSN 1487-3052 ; 25)
Includes bibliographical references and index.
ISBN 978-0-7766-0743-6

1. Administrative agencies—Customer services—Canada. 2. Consumer
satisfaction—Canada—Evaluation. 3. Electronic government
information—Canada. 4. Internet in public administration—Canada.
I. Dutil, Patrice A., 1960- II. Series: Governance series (Ottawa, Ont.) ; 25

JL86.C87S47 2010   351.71   C2010-902836-8

*For dedicated public servants
who shape and deliver services around the clock.*

TABLE OF CONTENTS

CONTRIBUTORS

Patrice Dutil is associate professor in the Department of Politics and Public Administration at Ryerson University.

Cosmo Howard is associate professor in the Department of Political Science and School of Public Administration at the University of Victoria.

John Langford is professor in the School of Public Administration at the University of Victoria.

Jeffrey Roy is associate professor in the School of Public Administration at Dalhousie University.

PREFACE

Although service improvement has long been on the public sector agenda, the advent of the Internet has greatly accelerated its importance as governments confront a more networked, instantaneous world where duplication and fragmentation are synonymous with dysfunction and dissatisfaction. A high profile review of service delivery mechanisms in the United Kingdom in 2006 (the Varney Review) provided this depiction:

> The Government historically delivers services through departments. The department might deliver the service directly, through agents or agencies, alone or in cooperation with local government. Each solution is a child of its time and circumstances, with little over-arching view of the Government's relationship with the citizen. Thus, I have found that departments which provide services focus predominantly not on the citizen, but on an aspect of the citizen called 'the customer'. This allows the department to focus on the delivery of their service – a transactional relationship.

> The end result is that the citizen who needs multiple services is left to join up the various islands of service to meet his or her needs. As departments do not appear to accept each other's identification of the citizen, the citizen has to validate his or her identity at each service transaction. This model of service provision is underpinned by a mass of helplines, call centres, front-line offices and websites. A similar situation applies to interactions with business resulting in business being required to provide the same information to many parts of government (Varney 2006: Foreword).

At about the same time Canada would lose its much-vaunted number one status according to the rankings by the global consultancy, Accenture.

Some of the early pioneering efforts at service innovation and online delivery on the part of the federal government—Government On-Line and Service Canada, for example—came to be increasingly the norm in terms of experimentation and initiative the world over. By the end of e-government's first full decade as mainstream, Canada would find itself decidedly in the middle of the pack of the world's most developed countries on many such scorecards—the United Nations Global Rankings, for example.

Invoking the need to move beyond the 'customer-driven transaction relationship' in the United Kingdom, echoing sentiments here in this country and elsewhere, Varney called for a shift to a more citizen-centric mindset—more holistic and relational and thus multi-faceted. While speed and efficiency signify success in a customer world, citizens can be called upon to play a role in selecting and designing services, and in providing oversight as to their impacts on individuals, companies and communities. The emergence of the next generation of the Internet, denoted as Web 2.0, personifies this shift toward a more participative ethos—at least for those online.

Governments, of course, deliver public services to many that prefer not to use the Web or are unable to do so—often an important distinction between the transactional world of the marketplace where customers are targeted and/or self-selected, and the realm of the state where the citizenry is all encompassing. In the latter case, clients may require a mix of online and in-person support, and the notion of the citizen denotes a political and civic dimension to the relationship between persons and their government(s). Indeed, governments in the plural is important since—while customers bemoan jurisdictional niceties—in federal jurisdictions such as Canada, the concept of citizenship, while often national in scope, also masks multiple relationships with multiple levels of government, each with their own interests and approaches in terms of involving the public in the service delivery process.

These are some of the main pieces of the puzzle that have come to define service transformation over the past decade. This book is an attempt to make sense of this fundamental recasting of both the purpose and form of public sector service delivery in a more multi-channel environment where the identities and interests of customers and citizens may not always easily align. There has nonetheless been ample experimentation in recent years to take stock of what has transpired—and more importantly, why. It is important to dig below the surface of the frontline glitz of portals and probe the inner workings of government in order to ascertain the consequences and implications of addressing Varney's depiction above which most everyone agrees needs redress and a significant degree of innovation if the public sector is to maintain a relevant, efficient and adaptable service apparatus.

Our voyage

This book is an accumulation of collaborative learning over the past five years among the book's authors and various stakeholders both inside and outside of the public sector. The effort has been driven by three converging threads of both conceptual and applied research: electronic government; public-private partnerships; and service transformation.

An important venue and starting point in this regard proved to be the annual Lac Carling meetings—a gathering of high-level officials from government and industry (and occasionally academe) devoted to the usage and deployment of information technologies in the public sector. While there are many facets to this theme, service transformation would emerge as the over-arching theme of much of Lac Carling's focus in recent years. This would be in keeping with Accenture's ranking of Canada as a global leader in e-government service delivery and various high level initiatives such as the 1999–2004 Government On-Line program—a precursor of sorts to the more encompassing Service Canada initiative as well as its more long-standing provincial cousins.

At these meetings in 2004 John Langford was invited to facilitate a dialogue on large scale service transformation initiatives involving collaborative efforts between industry and government. The interest generated by this session would lead to a collaborative effort between Langford, Patrice Dutil and Jeffrey Roy over the next year to produce a compilation of case studies for the 2005 meetings (where the results of the cases and their analysis were presented and discussed). During this time period Roy was on sabbatical at the University of Victoria collaborating with Langford on the nexus between e-government and public-private partnerships, as well as related initiatives that would bring Cosmo Howard into the fold. By the fall of 2005 this foursome would submit what would ultimately become a successful Social Sciences and Humanities Research Council (SSHRC) application resulting in a four year grant running from 2006–2009.

It is within this timeframe that the material presented was produced, disseminated, revised and ultimately distilled into this final product. Beyond Lac Carling, numerous other academic and applied venues were utilized in order gain insights into the topics presented—including annual Institute of Public Administration Canada (IPAC) meetings; various academic conferences; peer reviewed journals and books; and parallel projects involving the IBM Center for the Business of Government and the United Nations to name but a few. Moreover, in November 2007 the authors helped to orchestrate a conference hosted by Dalhousie University that would bring together some two hundred public servants from across the country as well as speakers from around the world. The conference was sponsored by the federal government's Service Canada and Nova Scotia's Service Nova Scotia and Municipal Relations.

The commonality of all of these meetings and outputs has been to both explore the multi-dimensional challenge that is public sector service transformation—including technology, organization, governance, culture, politics and citizenship, as well as to critically challenge much of the conventional wisdom put forth by service delivery leaders in government. Accordingly, the book is organized around a number of key questions pertaining to service innovation in a more digital and networked governance era. The questions are meant to probe the deeper meanings and consequences of what is being promised by service delivery proponents in government, as well as the implications for service recipients and stakeholders working within and along with public sector authorities.

While the authors have done their best to straddle and bridge both sides of the academic/applied divide, this particular book is meant first and foremost as a conceptual reflection on a hugely challenging and complex set of undertakings that have revamped much of how the government service apparatus now functions. While public servants—and in many cases their partners in industry—deserve praise for championing new reforms tied to more integrated service processes and better outcomes, our duty as neutral observers of these undertakings is to ask some basic questions about what has transpired and why, the results and impacts to date, and the key lessons learned for moving ahead. This last point reflects an underlying truth, which is that nothing remains static in today's environment where complacency is difficult to justify.

Yet in recent years in Canada there has arguably been a fair bit of complacency building on some early wins of high-profile initiatives such as Government On-Line and Citizens First surveys—initiatives that rightfully garnered much international praise for Canadian governments as leaders in the field. Canada would eventually lose its number one status granted by Accenture. Rankings by the United Nations and other institutions demonstrate a continual slippage in recent years of progress made—particularly as perceived by the all important citizen and as documented by one of Accenture's most recent surveys in 2007 that illustrated the gap between the government's own and the public's perception of performance. Questions need to be asked not only about whether progress has stalled in Canada but also about how performance is measured and defined in a world where fluid distinctions between customer and citizen relationships may not always be sufficiently recognized. Hopefully this book's inquisitions and propositions can thus better prepare tomorrow's service delivery champions with the cognitive capacities to think holistically and strategically about current contexts and how changes will unfold going forward.

Indeed, beyond those in the e-government and service communities at present, an important audience for this book are the public administration students of today that will become the public sector leaders of tomorrow. An appreciation of the intertwined dimensions of politics, organization, governance and technology is a precursor to navigating an environment where new service delivery channels are emerging at an accelerating pace and where the public expects to have a greater voice in service design, execution and evaluation.

Along with the Social Sciences and Humanities Research Council whose funding made this work possible, the authors are grateful to numerous public servants, colleagues and research assistants who took the time to partake in our dialogue and contribute to the development of this volume. They include: Peter Aucoin, Obbia Barni, Dan Belanger, Michelle Brady, Geoff Braun, Amanda Coe, Mark Jarvis, Evert Lindquist, Rob MacDonald, Nancy MacLellan, Jim McDavid, Gilles Paquet, Paul Thomas, Thea Vakil, and Ashley Walker. We would also like to thank the competent and thoughtful staff at the University of Ottawa Press, most especially McEvoy Galbreath and Anne Phillips. Unless otherwise noted, direct interviews conducted for this work were undertaken with the promise of anonymity and we must also acknowledge the helpful input of many blind reviewers who assessed portions of this text in more developmental stages. Despite the best efforts of all, any errors and omissions are nonetheless the sole responsibility of the authors.

While this work is the product of a splendid collaboration of colleagues, three of us owe a special debt to one of us. To the Robin Hood that was Jeffrey Roy in this project, we were merry men (a Little John, a Friar Tuck-albeit much leaner, and a Will "Scathelock" Scarlet). Jeffrey sparked the initiative, prodded it along with emails, calls, wisdom and encouragement. He ensured funding, travel, lodgings and wine. The alphabet that orders the names on the cover notwithstanding, Jeffrey spearheaded this initiative, and no preface would be complete without this recognition and expression of deep gratitude.

INTRODUCTION

Service Transformation in a Citizen-Centric World

A decade ago, service delivery was perceived as something done by trolls labouring at the bottom of impenetrable and boring 'line' departments—even the modifier 'line' suggests the tedium of production. Many public servants were trying to escape the world of front-line service delivery (metaphor: death in the trenches) to move into the trendier worlds of policy analysis and evaluation. This hardly encouraged new recruits to pursue a career in public service delivery.

All that has changed. Public servants want to be engaged in delivering public services. They are interested in the new service organizations like Service Nova Scotia, Service BC and Service Canada. They want to know how they can engage citizens in designing and developing services; they are fascinated by the collaborative efforts among service delivery departments to align or integrate complementary services; they want to explore the new multi-channel service delivery partnerships with IT firms; they are intrigued by new flexible approaches to procurement which make such partnerships possible and (we hope) successful; and they want to know more about the use of performance measurement tools to track success and enhance outcomes for citizens.

The renaissance of service delivery is the result of the influence of the very idea of 'service transformation'.

Obviously the notion of *improving* the delivery of public services is not new. In the 1980s and 90s, service improvement was largely focused on making simple, individual and self-contained transactional services more efficient and less expensive. The drivers were the service quality or total quality movements. Much of this work was done in the era of ruthless cost cutting and public sector downsizing and the models for improvement were drawn from the private manufacturing sector. In this world, privatization and private sector methods were good; public service was bad. This approach led to some solid successes in areas such as provision of drivers' licences, registry services, etcetera, and in some cases re-invigorated specific services and individual workplaces. But 1980s service improvement was not quite the stuff of which public service dreams are made.

By contrast, the more contemporary notion of 'service transformation' brings together a collection of ideas which together turns our normal approach to service delivery on its head. It opens up the possibility of:

- re-conceiving government services from the perspective of the citizen (or business), driving out service elements, rules and processes which add no public value and engaging the citizen or businesses in a variety of ways to do so—thus building public trust from the ground up with solid service improvements rather than overblown policy rhetoric;
- integrating or aligning complementary services (including internal government services) and working across agency, sectoral (i.e., private, not-for-profit) and jurisdictional (federal-provincial-municipal-First Nation) boundaries to do so;
- creating innovative and flexible partnerships with private sector firms to expand and integrate service channels including: face-to-face; phone, including text messaging; fax; mail; Internet portal for first contact; integrated information, forms and transaction opportunities (walk in, click-in, send in, phone in and thumb-in); and create secure systems for identification, authentication and electronic signatures which are accepted across departmental and governmental boundaries;
- redesigning the way the business of government is done, at least at the operational level, according to variations on a network model with a strong emphasis on collaboration, thus connecting service transformation to two of the most compelling governance trends of our time—the IT-based revolution in information and power and the engagement of community-based organizations in the delivery of public services; and
- reinvigorating government's commitment to performance measurement and management—focusing on service outcomes that

we can actually measure and creating data that can be used to tune service delivery plans.

It is this multi-faceted vision of citizen and business engagement; joined up services; multi-channel delivery; innovative partnering; collaborative networks; information sharing; and focus on outcomes and performance measurement, which lifts service transformation conceptually to a different plane than service improvement. It also makes service transformation one of the 'cool' things to be doing in the public sector at the moment.

Progress to date

Service transformation is not merely a dream. It is possible to point to developments in Canada reflecting the interplay of these concepts in the real transformation of the delivery of public services.

- There is the well-documented success of the dedicated service transformation corporation, Service New Brunswick. Other jurisdictions, including Nova Scotia, Quebec, Ontario, Alberta and British Columbia, have created centralized service transformation initiatives (e.g., Service Canada, ServiceOntario, etc.) which are less well known (Kernaghan 2008; Pardo and Dadayan 2006).
- There are also fascinating examples of service transformation at the municipal level, such as the 311 'single point of contact' service in Calgary, Toronto and Gatineau; the 211 service in Halton; and the integration of housing and family services in municipalities such as Winnipeg and Kingston.
- There are more limited signs of action on broader integration issues in areas such as social, health and security services: for example, the integrated social service delivery initiative for children with special needs (Community Living) in British Columbia (British Columbia 2009a).
- There are also early indicators of service integration crossing jurisdictional boundaries to enhance the provision of services to citizens and business:
  - o The Seniors Portal Network, integrating social services and health information from three levels of government;

o BizPaL, which provides Canadian businesses with one-stop access to permit and licence information for all levels of government, enabling business clients to do much of the permit and licence work themselves prior to contacting government;

o One stop, an integrated business registration and address change service involving the Province of British Columbia, the federal government and municipal governments in British Columbia.

- Finally there are infrastructure and 'back office' innovations designed to support the front end of service integration:

o The federal government's 'secure channel' suite of services was developed to provide individuals, businesses and government employees with secure and private access to all federal government online services; and

o The Canada Revenue Agency's business identifier number system—recognized by other federal government departments, municipal and provincial governments in several provinces—enables businesses to register electronically for multiple programs in multiple jurisdictions at one time.

And, lying behind almost all of these innovations, are the growing number of long term partnerships between Canadian governments and IT firms (Dutil, Langford and Roy 2005) designed to build multi-channel service delivery systems and the required back office systems for interoperability and secure transactions.

Getting behind the rhetoric

But when we look more closely, we see that the implementation of the service transformation vision is not without its problems and challenges. This book is about a number of these challenges. Specifically, it deals with six intriguing questions:

- Is it appropriate to treat citizens and clients as customers in the reform of public service delivery?
- Is 'satisfaction' an adequate measure of service improvement?
- Can we really 'transform' the culture in government service delivery agencies?

- Are governments successfully building the horizontal governance institutions and processes required to support service integration?
- Can our federal system support service integration across jurisdictional boundaries?
- Is our centrally-driven approach to service transformation out of step with emerging Web technologies?

Customers, clients and citizens

Chapter one asks the question: "What happened to the citizen?" This is a question posed by observers who notice our increasing reliance on simplistic customer relations management techniques that segment service users into large, often unhelpful, groups (seniors, immigrants, etc.) and seek feedback in unimaginative ways. At the level of rhetoric, the service recipient in 'citizen-centred' service has morphed from the 'customer' of the early private-sector oriented days of service improvement to the 'citizen'. In short, we all say 'citizen-centred' service. But, with too few exceptions, service users are still treated as rather simple-minded, generic 'customers' of individual agencies. Participative and interactive approaches to service design and decision making—which truly engage the service user—are rare. It is noteworthy that in some jurisdictions (e.g., the United Kingdom, and in particular, Scotland) customer relations management appears to be as much about citizen engagement as customer satisfaction, offering opportunities to the public not only to be surveyed about incremental delivery improvement but also creating new, more accessible consultation, reporting and accountability structures that truly engage the citizen in the design, delivery and monitoring of public services that matter to them. The continuous framing of the citizen as a generic customer represents the loss of an enormous 'people' opportunity which service transformation advocates, in most jurisdictions, should urgently re-address.

Many have argued that new electronic technologies have the potential to transform how governments relate to users of public services. Chapter one explores the limits of service transformation as it is being conceived by testing it against three service recipient models: customer, client and citizen. We argue that despite the opportunities that service transformations present for enhancing democratic citizen engagement and the power of clients, the market-inspired customer image is likely to remain the most powerful way in which service recipients are characterized and addressed. The 'business architecture' of service reform being installed today in the pursuit of better customer relationship management may also represent a decreasingly attractive medium for client empowerment and democratic interactions between service recipients and government.

Focusing on satisfaction

The service transformation movement is completely captured by the notion of enhancing customer 'satisfaction'. But as we become more familiar with the service revolution, we are bound to have some reservations about how the service transformation movement is measuring performance.

Is real performance measurement possible? Service transformation and performance measurement are joined at the hip. We promise stakeholders that we will be able to show that transforming the service delivery model will improve outcomes for citizens. But, after reading one too many self-serving, anecdotal case studies, you are bound to ask when the service transformation movement is going to grow up, leave the cheerleading behind, stop offering service transaction counts and simple process measures of citizen satisfaction (e.g., timeliness, accessibility, fairness, competence, etc.) and start focusing seriously on measuring performance? Simply put, are the anticipated policy outcomes of service integration being achieved? Does the cost of service integration exceed the benefits? Can we measure performance in complex environments involving multiple agencies and, potentially, many more factors influencing outcomes? Why are we so slow to develop useful outcome-oriented metrics for service users and other stakeholders? Can we calculate the value added by the large investments we are making in IT to increase and integrate service channels? These are tough questions, which we have largely been avoided to this point.

Chapter two begins this broader discussion by critically analyzing the methodologies associated with the customer satisfaction surveys broadly adopted by governments in Canada and elsewhere. Specifically, it examines the Citizens First survey tools and the Common Measurement Tool, attempting to establish whether these instruments create valid knowledge of the attitudes and preferences of public-service recipients. It points out significant shortcomings in the methodologies and opens up the wider question of how we might more effectively engage the service user in the assessment of service improvement initiatives.

Building a service culture

How do we build sustained employee engagement? Let's start by first recognizing the existence of service transformation 'champions', active service transformation 'communities of practice' (e.g., the Public Sector Service Delivery Council), pockets of huge enthusiasm and creativity in governments across Canada and plenty of new service training opportunities for front-line workers. At the same time, there is also considerable evidence that we have not made significant progress in broadly transforming the service culture at the operational and middle management levels. Efforts to align and integrate services are still plagued by hostile or defensive attitudes towards sharing information and power with potential partners. Building trust is the challenge here. For example, look at the problems we still face in breaking through cultural barriers separating firefighters, ambulance services, different police forces, coast guard, military personnel and intelligence services—all ostensibly working together in the joint provision of emergency, safety and security services. The challenge of deeply engaging employees in collaborative enterprises will only increase as we move beyond the easy integration projects and take on transformation projects involving harder policy problems, more entrenched stakeholders, and more complex technical infrastructure issues. Staff training is important, but trust is the foundation of a successful service transformation culture and building trust among employees from different units, ministries, governments and sectors remains a huge challenge bedeviling transformation initiatives in every jurisdiction.

Chapter three tackles this difficult question of culture change, looking critically at the efforts being made by Canadian governments to build service provider engagement and satisfaction as part of service transformation initiatives. Engagement and satisfaction have been identified in the private sector as key building blocks of a service culture. We argue that it is possible to promote a service culture in the public sector but that these efforts will be limited by factors unique to that sector.

Partnerships and horizontal governance

Partnerships are the glue of virtually all aspects of service transformation. They are used to avoid the inefficiency of departmental or even governmental re-organization when aligning or integrating related services offered by different units or agencies. They are also used to avoid the hazards of building internal technological support capacity by developing public-private partnerships with IT firms; and, similarly, to avoid internal service delivery shortcomings by building partnerships with community-based service delivery agencies.

But the immense dependency of the service transformation movement on partnerships raises important challenges related to: the vision of service integration; the sustainability of the collaborative governance model; and the capacity of governments to manage the complex relationships inherent in partnerships with big private sector firms.

Service transformation advocates exhort us to group service delivery around common service themes that are meaningful for citizens and businesses. But there seems to be little consensus in any particular jurisdiction (or across jurisdictions) about what those themes are, how far clustering should go and how we should organize ourselves to do it. Are we engaged in almost random 'bumper car integration' or do we have a deeper, more defensible view of how the pieces should fit together, and what the natural boundaries between service clusters are? If we have a vision, is it closely aligned with how service users and other stakeholders think the various service 'bubbles' should be joined together?

In some jurisdictions, we appear content to allow informal and loose partnerships aligning services among complementary service provision agencies to emerge in a *laissez-faire* manner. In other jurisdictions, we have created more centralized service transformation units. However, the mandate, partnership goals and authority of these centralized service organizations are often unclear. Are they supposed to become single service providers, facilitators of other service integrators or merely single window portal managers providing information and redirecting citizens and businesses to other transactional venues? Why are some service delivery areas included in their mandates and others excluded?

But service transformation driven partnerships don't end at the borders of government departments. Long term relationships with IT firms—or even consortia of large IT firms—are a key feature of almost all major service transformations. In the past, major service-transformation IT projects often failed catastrophically and the investigations that followed pointed to the lack of clearly established responsibilities among the partners and the inadequacies of accountability mechanisms.

Chapter four considers the governance challenges emerging from these new service networks. Successful collaborative or network governance is a key building block of service transformation. We rhetorically rally around the idea of shifting away from a model of hierarchical direct service delivery to one of networked government using a web of government agencies and private sector and non-profit partners—the so-called value delivery network—to transform service delivery. But the cultural challenges to collaboration at the operational level (noted earlier) are often accented by our ambivalent attitude towards this vision of joined up governance. We profess to be devoted to collaboration but continue to support hierarchically-oriented goal setting, service planning, decision making, resourcing and monitoring systems that encourage isolation and competition rather than partnership. Building in shared accountability for outcomes is a particularly vexing governance challenge, especially where the partnerships cross departmental or sectoral boundaries.

Service transformation across jurisdictional boundaries

If we look beyond individual jurisdictions, the vision is even muddier. Except for some early work on standards for identity authentication and advances in a few narrow program areas (e.g., tax collection), Canadian governments have as yet provided little collective leadership or institutional support for boundary spanning integration initiatives. This represents a significant challenge for service transformation in a federal state with constitutional division of powers and robust municipal governments, raising difficult questions about interoperability and the future of federated service architecture.

Chapter five examines the efforts being made to extend service integration across levels of government in Canada and other countries. It points out the innovative steps that have been taken at the bureaucratic level, but also reflects on both the absence of political leadership and the invisibility of these initiatives in the mainstream academic dialogue concerning the evolution of federalism. The former situation is particularly concerning. In Canada service transformation mostly flies below the political radar. Politicians may be there for the ribbon snipping when a new initiative is announced but they are much less of a presence at moments when barriers between departments or governments need to be dismantled to implement the next service integration or alignment.

Service transformation and technology

Service transformation is a movement increasingly fueled by technological innovation. What was once characterized as 'e-government'—a discreet initiative of many governments—has become central to the strategy of service transformation in all Canadian jurisdictions. Technology has been the driver of multi-channel delivery systems, service integration, customer management systems and the back office architecture that powers contemporary service transformation. The network model derived from modern electronic technology has become the driver of service system governance reform.

However, technology may be moving faster than the service transformation movement which it fuels. Chapter six explores the implications of the rise of Web 2.0 for service reform. It points out the potential for increasing friction between the demands of mass collaboration; interdependence and choice; and the capacities of still hierarchically-organized governments to adapt to these demands. This discussion picks up a number of the service transformation themes raised in previous chapters (citizen engagement, cultural change, governance and performance measurement) and speculates about their future in a Web 2.0 world.

An overarching question

Overall, this book asks the question: "Is service transformation on a successful trajectory?" Observers are initially impressed by Canada's high standings over the years in the service transformation league tables, but then wonder why we seem to be so reluctant to move beyond service transformation initiatives which integrate information and allow for the simplest service transactions. In short, they tumble to the idea that service transformation movements in many jurisdictions have picked the 'low hanging fruit' but seem to be having trouble moving to the next level, integrating or aligning more complex interactive services. We ask if we are 'missing the boat' on key issues such as citizen engagement, performance measurement, cultural change, governance reform and technological adaptation. More technically inclined observers also wonder if the development of the back end of the service transformation infrastructure will be able to keep up with developments and demands at the front end. Are governments ready to take on this less glamorous work, putting serious resources into building a holistic infrastructure to facilitate interoperability among potential partners—a service-oriented architecture that maximizes opportunities for exchange and re-use of information without compromising security and privacy protection?

In posing such questions, we are really getting at something more basic. We want to know if the service transformation movement has peaked. Have we lost our energy for pursuing citizen-centred service and are we sliding back into the more comfortable and traditional 'deliverer-oriented' service delivery? In the end is it just about saving money? One student observer focused attention on an advertisement for a recent service transformation summit in London, which proclaimed that "every case study presented demonstrates either a 20 percent cashable savings or a 20 percent increase in standards of service delivery." He wanted to know if participants would be more interested in the former or the latter. To misquote B. B. King, "the thrill may not be gone" but the honeymoon is certainly over. We need to look hard at the progress we have made, the vision we are embracing and the steps we need to take to make sure that this exciting idea doesn't slip below the bureaucratic waves.

CHAPTER ONE

Serving Whom: Customers, Clients or Citizens?

As suggested in the introduction, service transformation encapsulates a complex and somewhat disjointed collection of reforms. It is driven by multiple objectives such as increasing responsiveness to the public; enhancing efficiency and value for money; improving access and convenience; protecting fairness; and increasing administrative competence and effectiveness. Furthermore, many strategies have been implemented in the pursuit of these ends, including clustering, integration, personalization, e-delivery, tele-servicing, co-production and alternative service delivery. Clearly service transformation does not represent a straightforward and coherent administrative reform agenda, but is rife with ambiguities, dilemmas, tensions and contradictions.

Complexity, confusion and contradiction are familiar features of public administration, but it may be surprising to learn that service transformation, with its promise to simplify and streamline government services, can itself be a source of administrative ambiguity and inconsistency. In this chapter we suggest that the relative emphasis placed on different service transformation goals and strategies has varied across sectors and jurisdictions, and that these variations have had profound implications for the ways in which the public experiences public services. We claim it is possible and useful to categorize service transformation efforts according to how they imagine the identity of the service-user. The three most important identities are *customer*, *client* and *citizen*. In Canada, these different terms are in play but governments to date have not systematically considered their distinctly different meanings. Yet, understanding the different service-user identities allows us to highlight and critically reflect upon key trends in Canadian service transformation.

We argue public service users are increasingly perceived and treated in Canada as customers, with lessening regard to the potential importance of client and citizen relationships. There are two underlying reasons for such a claim, both underpinning our examination of the nuance and consequences of different imaginings of the service user. The first reason is that the public service has led the service delivery revolution in Canada and it has seemed more comfortable treating the public as end-consumers of public services rather than as clients or citizens (see chapter two). The second reason is that elected officials or politicians have rarely championed the role of citizens, or indeed of clients, in this transformation of government. As a result, and despite new opportunities that service transformation presents for enhancing democratic citizen engagement and the power of clients, it is the 'customer' that is likely triumphant, but with little regard for the implications for the broader credibility, responsiveness and performance of democratic governance.

It is our contention that this trend is unsustainable and has the potential to produce significant unintended consequences. Accordingly, this chapter seeks to ignite the theoretical debate in Canada over how service recipients should be 'seen' by service providers in an era in which information and communications technology open up so many different opportunities for engagement. The chapter is organized in the following manner. First, we briefly probe three images of the service recipient—customer, client and citizen. The three sections that follow explore the political, administrative and technological contexts of service transformation and the respective images of the public service recipient as customer, client and citizen. We set out the provenance of each characterization, provide examples of the image as it is articulated by its key advocates, and analyze some key issues raised by more vigorous pursuit of each model.

'Customer' service and service integration

The logic of customer-centric governance, rooted in private sector managerial practises, was championed by advocates of the new public management (NPM), an approach best captured by Osborne and Gaebler's *Reinventing Government* (1992). Based largely on the experiences of state and local governments in the United States, the book lauded attempts to create more decentralized managerial structures across a public sector and trumpeted efforts made in improving customer service outcomes via efficient organizational processes. The terminology of 'customer' came to represent an approach to public administration preoccupied with enhancing convenience and choice for service users—one in which the relationship between publics and public services was made up of transactional exchanges (see chapter two).

With respect to public administration, the term 'agency' is central to the evolution of NPM as a means of organizational restructuring within the public sector (Pollitt et al. 2004). Yet the agency movement represents contradictory pressures in the context of customer-centric service transformation. On the one hand, agencies have been proposed to promote specialization, flexibility and responsiveness to local customer groups, moving away from standardized, one-size-fits-all models. The United Kingdom's early pursuit of executive agencies in the late 1980s reflected the decentralizing flavour of NPM reforms: more autonomous and empowered units better able to serve their customer base in innovative ways ideally freed from the shackles of centralized administrative control. Whereas the United Kingdom and New Zealand went furthest in embracing agency-based mentality, the Canadian experience federally (and to a large extent provincially) consisted of some modest experiments during the late 1980s with so-called 'special operating agencies' (very similar to the United Kingdom's 'executive agencies'), a status that continues to this day with bodies such as the Passport Office and Parks Canada. Though still politically accountable to, and embedded within larger ministerial departments or portfolios, these units were given a modest increase in managerial freedom (primarily in terms of budgeting and business planning) in order to improve efficiency and service outcomes for end-users. Borrowing what had then been an exclusively private sector practice, such units even began to report annually on their financial and business performance as a means of demonstrating results.

But there is a second contradictory set of customer service imperatives pushing the creation of agencies. This is the movement for integrated one-stop-shops, justified on the grounds that the 'customer' prefers to obtain all their services from government in one convenient (real or virtual) location. Agency-driven service integration of this kind is found in prominent and influential examples like Australia's Centrelink and Service New Brunswick (SNB). Here the focus is on harmonization and standardization of delivery systems, and the agency model (theoretically) allows programs developed in disparate ministries to be merged into a single, seamless service interface.

This business stylization reinforced the customer-service logic of public sector restructuring just as the Internet emerged as a powerful new venue for efficient and simplified transactional encounters in the marketplace. Online banking and electronic commerce captured the attention of early government proponents of electronic service delivery. Initiatives such as the annual e-government survey by Accenture Consulting and Canadian Citizens First series (see chapter two) explicitly emphasized the customer service dimension of public sector performance. Indeed, the growing reliance on private sector specialists to realize e-government reforms has reinforced the business mentality and, often, the placement of industry personnel within authority structures devoted to technology that have augmented in recent years, both in Canada and elsewhere.

The most significant example of customer service-inspired reforms at the federal level in Canada has been the transformation of Revenue Canada from a traditional department employing approximately forty thousand people into a uniquely specialized agency—the Canada Customs and Revenue Agency that has since become simply the Canada Revenue Agency (CRA). The experiment went much further than previous Canadian special operating agencies by formally segmenting political oversight and accountability (via a minister) and managerial and operational responsibilities that have been uniquely and publicly vested in an appointed official (chief commissioner) who, in turn, accounts to a board. As it pursued its own business-inspired corporate governance model, Australia became an important benchmark for the CRA. For example, the creation of Centrelink in the 1990s represented Australia's flagship service improvement effort—one that has since been an important reference point for Service Canada—reflecting its intention to inject a customer service mentality into its delivery operations, and to become much more technologically sophisticated in doing so (Vardon 2000). Centrelink has since endured numerous growing pains in terms of governance structures, organizational culture and performance outcomes, in part due to the managerial and political complexities of its set of 'client' relationships in the realms of social assistance and human services. The distinction between customer and client is returned to below, along with further discussions pertaining to Centrelink.

In Canada, the CRA would prove no less influential in pursuing a customer-focused agenda, one that would become well suited for online adaptation as Internet usage grew rapidly in the late 1990s. In fact, with its highly successful e-filing initiatives which offer individual Canadians the opportunity to file their tax return online—a channel that co-exists with others, notably traditional forms and telephone-based completion—CRA became the Government of Canada's flagship performer in terms of online transactional services. The uptake of e-filing has recently surpassed the fifty percent mark of Canadian taxpayers, an impressive achievement reflecting not only convenience but also a growing level of public confidence in the security of infrastructure for doing so (for a document with considerable amounts of confidential information). Despite the rather unfriendly persona of CRA as a tax collector, as an agency it has made considerable effort to improve its customer service capacities, not only in terms of offering new online channels, but also with respect to benchmark response times to external inquiries (aligning benchmarks across service channel); improving the knowledge and skills of front-line staff; and communicating its results in a business-like fashion with annual reports detailing both objectives and results (Roy 2006a).

In parallel to CRA's efforts, the federal Government On-Line (GOL) initiative was first introduced in 1999 as an ambitious effort not only to move all government services online (a goal that was later revised to include all 'essential' services), but also to repackage these service offerings in a more customer-friendly manner. Thus, the much lauded Government of Canada portal featured three clusters or service streams of distinct types of information and transactions (Canadians, businesses and the awkwardly named non-Canadians, for potential visitors and new entrants). The creation of Internet portals with integrated service streams based on usage patterns such as life events (as opposed to departmental structures) further reflects a customer segmentation mentality, perhaps less rooted in NPM than its more recent cousin, the equally industry-oriented customer relationship management (CRM). Today the literature on e-government and service reform efforts is replete with references to CRM in the public sector, although more nuanced observers have made the point that citizenship orientation of government may hinder the appropriateness and applicability of business-style CRM in government, a theme further explored below (Schellong and Goethe 2006).

The need for government-wide mechanisms to foster technical interoperability, information exchange and coordinated managerial action can induce pressures for centralized authority that counter to some degree the initial flow of NPM away from the centre toward more autonomous, decentralized units (as demonstrated by examples such as CRA and Centrelink). The resulting need for a 'federated architecture' is thus central to both integrating and coordinating service delivery capacities (Batini et al. 2002). The fundamental question and challenge that lies at the heart of governance reform—and new, more integrated and multi-channel service delivery capacities in particular—is whether this federated architecture will be sought through centralized mechanisms to impose interoperability through vertical hierarchy (i.e., traditional public sector authority from central agencies and individual ministers empowered to ordain organizational change) or rather via more novel and networked governance mechanisms that are more collaborative and diffused in terms of their accountability relationships (Reed 2004; Kamarck 2004).

Struggling with 'client' relations

The term *client* is, at times, used as a contemporary synonym for *customer*. But it is possible to apply the term in a more careful manner to describe specifically those individuals who depend on assistance and support provided through government human and social service social systems. In many cases, users of these services are vulnerable and depend on the care, guidance and support provided by expert human service providers. These users often develop long term relationships with service providers and the service relationship is frequently asymmetrical, especially where providers have the legal and professional authority to impose decisions and withhold supports. This asymmetry is exacerbated where the service recipients lack, or are deemed to lack, the necessary emotional, intellectual or physical capacities. The range of services that fall under this category of service delivery is very broad and includes: health care; jails and penitentiaries; housing services; income assistance and employment support; public guardianship; social work services for children, families and youth; special education programs; and various supports for persons with intellectual, physical and psychiatric disabilities. Perceived in this manner, the term 'client' conjures up a host of complex ideas about democratic engagement, especially in the context of contemporary e-government oriented service transformation.

A consistent theme running through the literature on human services is the suggestion that client-based service delivery should be 'democratized'. The democratization of client-based service delivery places specific demands on service organizations. A critical condition is the development of partnership or 'collegiality' between clients and workers (Hardina 2005; Leon 1999), which means that clients need to be directly involved in decision making about the design and production of services. This involves clients in more than just providing feedback to inform internal decision making. Closely related to this is the need for service provision to be structured in such a way that enables clients and workers to develop relationships of mutual understanding, respect and trust, which requires that work is coupled in a client-centred way—that is, staff organize their work around their individual clients, not according to specialized functions (Hubberstey 2001; Leon 1999; Skrtic, Sailor and Gee 1996). Some authors argue that service must be integrated, in order to be effective and properly take into account the needs and priorities of the 'whole client' (Hubberstey 2001; Leon 1999). However, others note that multiple entry points or 'pathways' are valuable, since they offer choices and service alternatives where one service deliverer has failed to work effectively with the client (McLennan et al. 2003).

Some commentators argue that democratic service organizations must be internally democratic. Employees at all levels need to be included in decision making, believe their judgment is valued, and feel they have supervisory support to engage clients democratically. They must have discretion to deal flexibly with individuals (Yeatman and Owler 2001) and they require additional administrative resources, including information technology, and more time and training in new techniques. Skrtic, Sailor and Gee argue that if human service organizations are to be responsive to their clients, they also need to develop internal adaptability and flexibility. They reject both traditional 'machine bureaucracies' and professional bureaucracies in favour of 'adhocracy', in which teams of staff collaborate and share information in order to build on the insights gained from practice (Skrtic, Sailor and Gee 1996).

While such client-centric orientations have often been overshadowed in recent decades by the customer mindset of the new public management (Sossin 2002), their influence can be found in several contemporary initiatives. In Australia and the United Kingdom the democratization of social service delivery is central to public service transformation strategies. As noted, Centrelink is the Australian government's flagship service delivery agency and has, since 1997, delivered integrated social services across the country. It aims to provide personalized service that is tailored to an individual user's needs and to encourage choice and voice so that users can select from alternative services and negotiate program conditions (Vardon 2000; Howard 2003, 2006). The agency instituted several reforms, including the One-to-One Service Initiative and the Personal Adviser Program, to facilitate the development of ongoing relationships between service users and staff. Centrelink has also invested heavily in e-service delivery through online information facilities and also integrated data management, which allows staff rapidly to access case information. The agency automated a number of front-line activities, including the assessment of job seekers with special needs, as well as the management of referrals and client sanctioning procedures (Henman and Adler 2003; Howard 2003, 2006). These reforms also featured the NPM themes of funding reduction and expectations of efficiency improvements (Mulgan 2003).

By contrast, the British government led by then Prime Minister Tony Blair substantially increased the level of funding for government human services after taking office in 1997. In its early years, the New Labour administration sought to differentiate its social service agenda from previous managerial type reforms by pouring new resources into service delivery and embracing the goals of social inclusion and participation as part of a broader concern with social disadvantage and marginalization (Barnett 2002). Blair's promotion of 'choice, voice and personalization' in the context of public service delivery was part of a strategy to use service transformation to link the government's social inclusion and participation agendas into a broader model of democratic citizen engagement (Blair 2006; Cutler, Wayne and Brevony 2007; Hutton 2006). A good example of this is the 'Connecting Britain' e-government strategy, which seeks to contribute to improved computer literacy amongst digitally and socially marginalized citizens (United Kingdom 2005). In contrast to many other Anglo jurisdictions, the UK rhetoric makes frequent mention of the need to empower and support front-line staff. The Scottish Executive's 2006 *Transforming Public Services* strategy makes similar connections between the broad service transformation agenda and the specific needs of disadvantaged service users (Scottish Executive 2006). The Scottish government stresses several common themes, including one-window service, community participation, the need to respond on an individual basis to the needs of clients, the importance of productivity and the potential for new technologies to facilitate the joining up of organizations, jurisdictions and programs (Ibid.).

The association of client-centred service with mainstream service transformation agendas has aided the democratization of client service in these jurisdictions in several ways. While there is limited empirical research on the impact of recent service delivery reforms, both Australia and the United Kingdom have created formal structures to allow client input and enhance user accountability through complaints mechanisms, new appeal structures, legislated user-consultation requirements and client-satisfaction research programs (Ibid.; Vardon 2000). In both countries, new resources have been provided to human service delivery systems in order to support attention to individual needs. Computer technology has also been used in Australia to streamline and automate several income support functions, resulting in more consistent and accurate application of rules in certain areas, as well as greater consistency and comprehensiveness of information contained in the system, which permits the agency to offer more effective multi-channel service delivery (Howard 2006).

Along with the potential benefits of such automation have come new problems and tensions, particularly for the organizational and managerial structures shaping relations between public servants and clients. In both Australia and the United Kingdom, the autonomy of many human service professionals has been reduced through attempts to codify and categorize the competencies they require to complete their work and to quantify and measure the outcomes of professional intervention. This has led in some contexts to a 'Taylorization' of care work, which has enabled and, in turn, been reinforced by the automation of many functions, as well as the transfer of tasks from professionals to clerks (Foster and Wilding 2000; Henman and Adler 2003). It is likely that such changes have reduced the ability of local staff to respond to a user's needs on an individualized basis. Though these trends are most visible in Australia, New Zealand and the United Kingdom, they have also been observed in several Canadian provinces (Baines 2004). The recent shift in the United Kingdom towards a rhetorical emphasis on front-line staff and their needs suggests some reversal of this trend (Blair 2006).

The tendency to impose transactional or market models of customer choice and exit on social services is illustrated in the Australian Job Network. In this NPM-inspired system, the government contracts with a collection of private and not-for profit organizations to provide employment services for disadvantaged job seekers across the country. It deliberately funds multiple providers in order to encourage competition and choice. The government rewards providers financially when they place an unemployed client in a paid position. The providers have an incentive to park difficult cases and concentrate on those easiest to place (Considine 2001). Furthermore, the time spent interacting and building relationships with clients has fallen since the introduction of the quasi-market for employment services in 1998. While there is evidence that the new system is more effective at placing job seekers in employment, this example illustrates some of the pitfalls of NPM-inspired models of social service reform from the perspective of democratization. The institutionalized emphasis on easily measurable and quantifiable outcomes and the payment of rewards for performance has encouraged service providers to reduce the time they spend with users and to focus on short term employment results rather than working with clients to discover their individual needs and aspirations and develop their abilities and skills (Ibid.).

While cost reduction is not a universal trend in contemporary social service reform, the widespread emphasis on reducing costs and improving efficiency has produced overstretched systems where excessively large caseloads do not permit staff to get to know clients, or to work with them for a sufficient length of time to achieve the desirable outcomes associated with service democratization (Howard 2003, 2006). High levels of staff turnover undermine relationship building and are serious problems in public services such as Canada's, which are suffering poor morale as a result of periods of downsizing and continual political assaults on the legitimacy of government service provision (Bakvis 2000). The focus on efficiency has encouraged the transfer of functions from trained care workers to front-line clerks who are less likely to have professional affiliations or qualifications, suggesting they are less likely to resist the commands and demands of superiors or possess the skills to communicate and collaborate with vulnerable clients (see chapter three). Despite the positive effects of computerization such as information sharing for more integrated service offerings and significant amounts of information available online, automation has also empowered management at the expense of front-line workers and service users, and has shifted the focus from intangible service outcomes to measurable outputs (Henman and Adler 2003).

Engaging the 'citizen'

In the context of these contrary assessments, we turn to an analysis of the challenges facing those who would exploit the potential of service transformation to contribute to a broader strengthening of the democratic potential of service recipients and other individuals in the community as citizens. The most obvious starting point is that service recipients prefer to have themselves characterized as *citizens*. In a recent Government of Canada survey, for instance, 48 percent of respondents indicated that they prefer to be thought of as citizens when receiving services. Being thought of as a client (16 percent) or customer (13 percent) ranks far behind and even below the category of taxpayer (19 percent) (Ekos Research Associates 2006). These kinds of results are reinforced by more general Crossing Boundaries survey findings which indicate that three out of five Canadians want more direct influence on government decision making between elections (Hume 2006).

Many interesting questions arise from such findings. Who do such survey respondents include within the meaning of 'citizen'? Would citizens actually take advantage of greater opportunities to be involved in government planning, decision making, implementation and monitoring around service transformation? Thus, a central question is what it might mean to be characterized as a citizen in the context of engaging with government as part of a service transformation initiative.

Undoubtedly, the most robust citizen engagement model would be deliberative democracy. This model transcends the democratic opportunities contemplated by customer or client interaction models and sees service transformation as an opportunity to engage citizens (both affected and interested others) in a comprehensive dialogue (with service providers and other citizens) on the nature of the service being provided and the means being used to deliver it. From the democratic theory perspective, this model also transcends representative and pluralist models of democracy, contemplating participation opportunities beyond the information sharing and consultation activities available under the latter models (Norris 2003). The Organisation for Economic Co-operation and Development (OECD) characterizes this as the 'active participation' model, differentiating it from 'information' and 'consultation' relationships (OECD 2001).

To qualify as 'active participative', 'deep' or 'deliberative', citizen engagement would have to be focused on formative dialogue about what to do, rather than merely an assertion of wants or needs in response to survey or focus group questions. Such engagement would also be based on comprehensive, balanced and accessible information; take place at points in time in which the agenda is still open to expansion and revision; and use deliberative 'spaces' and institutional arrangements that allow for an orderly interaction and collaboration without prejudice among the widest possible range of affected stakeholders (Coleman and Gøtze 2003; Lukensmeyer and Torres 2006).

Various governments and citizen-centred service advocates have signalled that more robust forms of citizen engagement should be part of the service transformation package. Unfortunately, the data on the degree to which governments at all levels are actually providing significant engagement opportunities as part of their e-government initiatives is spotty (Scott 2006). In its e-government vision, the New Zealand government highlights the democratic potential of service transformation, indicating that the implementation of e-government will make it easier for people to have their say in government. The New Zealand service transformation vision references the opportunities for citizens to interact with ministry officials to affect policy, indicating that this will enhance participation and build public trust (New Zealand 2000). Similarly, the UK government recently outlined its plans for administrative transformation through new technologies in a service-oriented manner consistent with a strong customer emphasis (i.e., highly transactional services with strong potential for electronic delivery). It established that one of its performance objectives was that citizens feel more engaged with the process of democratic government (United Kingdom 2005). This objective is reinforced—as noted above—by the dual strategy of 'voice' and 'choice' that is increasingly part of the service transformation debate in the United Kingdom (United Kingdom 2006a).

Similar claims are evident in the rhetoric of service transformation initiatives of governments across Canada. The federal government's Online Advisory Panel, for instance, made "engaging citizens more fully in governance processes, not just at election time, but throughout the governance cycle that runs from policy formulation to program planning, service delivery, and performance evaluation" one of the primary challenges of the federal e-government service transformation initiatives (Canada 2003). Many Canadian provincial governments have also recently made commitments to provide regularly updated information about patient wait-times across health care providers.

There are other cases of one-off experiments with electronic democratic engagement at the departmental levels of national and provincial level governments, but not all of the most prominent examples are directly related to service transformation. The Canadian Department of Foreign Affairs and International Trade, for instance, hosted an online discussion forum as part of its 2003 foreign policy review. In another well documented case, the US Environmental Protection Agency created a substantial national online dialogue about its draft public involvement policy (Beierle 2002). In the related world of regulation, the US federal government's e-rulemaking initiative is opening up the prospect of substantial online public engagement in the development of rules by federal agencies pursuant to legislation (Carlitz and Gunn 2005).

The opportunity for significant democratization seems strongest to some in circumstances in which voluntary sector organizations are involved in the new service delivery mix. The findings of the Edelman Trust Barometer, an annual survey that measures public opinion on matters of institutional trust across a range of countries, can be instructive in this regard (Edelman 2006). They demonstrate that whereas both industry and government have suffered from a decline in perceptions of legitimacy and trustworthiness in recent years, confidence in non-governmental organizations has risen sharply. One explanation for this rise is the more participatory nature of civil society organizations and evidence suggesting that in today's world, a key determinant of trust is that of a horizontal relationship between individuals and organizations, more peer-based, networked in nature and less rooted in deference to authority, hierarchy and top-down design of services. It is arguable that service transformations that engage civil society organizations are likely to present affected individuals and groups with more opportunities (electronic and face-to-face) to interact in a democratic manner with service providers. By way of example, a recent Crossing Boundaries report draws attention to initiatives to bring local citizens into processes designed to create community consensus on what priorities and outcomes the community wants from public investment and programs (Hume 2006).

Why would we even consider trying to hang such weighty forms of democratic engagement on what many observers might prefer to see as merely an efficient way to repackage public services for customers and clients?

This is an interesting question that merits careful consideration. The basic argument in favour of this vision of deep democratization of service transformation begins with the observation that most of the other democratic opportunities available to citizens within our form of representative democracy are severely compromised (at least at the federal and provincial levels) by forces such as executive domination, party propaganda and the power of special interest groups. As a result, citizens increasingly shun traditional forms of democratic participation and their mistrust of political processes continues to grow. But, by necessity, citizens continue to avail themselves of state services and generally exhibit more positive attitudes towards service providers than politicians. Therefore, the reinvention of those services, even though conducted largely in a bureaucratic setting, provides a potentially powerful opportunity to engage the citizen, not just as a client or customer, but as an important participant in the wider governance process.

The role of public servants as facilitators of deliberative democratic engagement is part of a long-established (if regularly suppressed) thread of public administration theory which sees public servants as proactive interpreters of the public interest (Kernaghan and Langford 1990). Not only do public servants have motive, then, but they also have opportunity.

The role of interpreting or balancing interests places obligations on public servants to consult closely with citizens—an obligation that is facilitated by their location at the nexus of electronic governance. Whatever the role of politicians in service transformation (and it is usually pretty limited), it is public servants working out the details who control and make use of the contemporary tools of interaction such as the electronic town hall, the listserv, or interactive websites and games. Public servants run the ministry websites that provide information, report on results and solicit the reaction of citizens to draft plans and results. Politicians are not only missing in action with respect to service transformation but they are also—certainly in Canada—running way behind public servants in adapting to the interactive potential of the Internet to work out shared public preferences with respect to public services.

While some governments and citizen-centric service advocates show enthusiasm for deliberative democracy opportunities associated with service transformation initiatives, the further development of this type of public engagement faces serious challenges.

First, while we can find some evidence of governments embracing more robust forms of democratic engagement in the course of service transformations, we can probably find more evidence of democratic rhetoric masking a customer approach to engagement. Being 'citizen-centred' still does not mean comprehensively engaging the citizen in the design, implementation and oversight of service transformations.

Second, if the increasing interactivity of service delivery did spill over into the provision of deeper democratic engagement in the design, development, implementation and oversight of electronic service transformations then we would have to pay closer attention to equality of access. The digital divide may be diminishing somewhat in many jurisdictions but it can still create or perpetuate different levels of political influence. The evidence from some online dialogue initiatives is that they tend to be dominated by individuals representing the same organizations that would traditionally dominate policy debate in that sector (Beierle 2002).

Third, despite some academic advocacy for a more proactive engagement role for public servants in the name of balancing interests and protecting rights, there is also a solid thread of contrary argument which insists that public servants should not be taking the lead in interacting with citizens when the dialogue moves beyond exchanging information and answering questions. Service transformation is often policy change by stealth. There is considerable anecdotal evidence from the front lines of service improvement of politicians feeling strong pressures to change policy to catch up with the demands of citizens and service providers who, after much interaction, share a collective vision of how a service should be transformed.

Fourth, research on service-based public engagement, both electronic and face-to-face, is still extremely rudimentary. This is an area in which more careful work is required to clarify the engagement intentions of service transformation initiatives and document the reality and rhetoric associated with their implementation. In addition, such research would provide an opportunity to determine the degree to which the increase in citizen trust and confidence in government that service improvements appear to generate (Heintzman and Marson 2005) is affected by the level of citizen engagement in the service transformations themselves.

Imagining service transformation—a lost opportunity?

Canadian public administration's self-image is of pragmatism and restraint (Gow 2004). Whereas other jurisdictions embraced reform programs like new public management with ideological fervour, Canadians like to think of themselves as resisting ideological excesses and sampling strategically from the different administrative approaches on offer (Aucoin 2002). In the field of service delivery, this reluctance to fully embrace fashions is evident in several areas: we have shown much less enthusiasm for 'agencification', outsourcing and privatization than was found in the United Kingdom and New Zealand; we have refrained from radically shaking up human services in the way Australia and the United Kingdom have; and we have arguably eschewed the more extreme characterizations of service users as customers, such as those found in Clinton and Gore's Reinventing Government agenda. In contrast, some argue that Canada adopts a more nuanced view of the role of the public service—one that accepts trade-offs and limitations—and is willing to confront the ambiguities and complexities associated with treating service users as citizens (Ibid.). This being said, advocates of citizen-centred service in Canada have not been immune to fervour; they have aggressively and systematically championed their vision of service transformation domestically and internationally, portraying Canada as a world leader on the cutting edge of service transformation. Yet the self-perception of these advocates has never been of zealous crusading in the name of an ideological agenda.

Rather, service transformation is presented as politically uncontroversial, policy-neutral and simply an objective reflection of what the public wants (see chapter two).

We have seen in this chapter that service transformation is controversial. It represents a complex mix of agendas and objectives, many of which conflict with each other as well as other important aspects of public administration and policy. The service reform programs proposed by advocates are contested in multiple ways by multiple actors. There is not one universal model of service delivery that works in all service settings. Governments have imagined the users of government services in multiple ways—customers, clients and citizens. Yet the failure to explicitly and systematically consider the implications of these different imaginings has had important consequences for the trajectory of Canadian service transformation. Most significantly, it has facilitated the gradual extension of customer relationships in the public sector and a noticeable crowding out of client and citizen models.

The advent of the Internet and digital technologies is without doubt an important dimension of today's governance complexities and the range of customer, client and citizen-based relationships at play. Whereas the notion of e-government began (chronologically) for most governments as an opportunity for online service delivery, embracing a customer-driven philosophy inspired by electronic commerce, it has also become increasingly apparent that such a direct transfer from the commercial to the political realm is simplistic and unworkable. The reasons for such a claim are nestled in the preceding analysis, demanding a more sophisticated appreciation of how technology impacts the different realms of customer, client and citizen relations. The manner by which e-government has been pursued in many jurisdictions carries important consequences here. The fact that much of the technology management apparatus of the public sector is typically orchestrated for a customer service and communications mentality—as opposed to one more open to consultation and engagement—is an important factor.

What seems apparent from transformational efforts of the past decade is that although the advent of e-government has reinforced the logic of 'customer' service interlinked with a widening CRM–NPM organizational nexus, the managerial and political implications of this nexus for the public sector are more complex. Regarding the political aspects of such changes, the rise of new aspirations from within the citizenry and new promises by government leaders for e-democracy and more innovative and direct forms of public engagement is a case in point. It is difficult to find a government today that is not claiming to be pursuing opportunities for citizen engagement, many of which involve online channels and tools.

Whether or not the 'business architecture' being developed by governments to better deliver services to customers is suitable for new forms of engagement is questionable. Although there have been pockets of success in terms of direct service application to customer-inspired delivery models (such as online tax filing, for instance, where the uptake has been remarkable), most aspects of government operations have proven to be multi-faceted across policy objectives, delivery channels and the means for integrating the two. One notable result has been a much more 'client-centric' focus of public-private partnering where successful collaborative models involve high levels of stakeholder engagement and collaborative learning in order to generate value (Dutil, Langford and Roy 2005).

The engagement of the service recipient can also be considered through this client prism in terms of the manner by which the creation and extension (or contraction) of multiple delivery channels enables more autonomy or self-empowerment on the part of the public. This point may involve not only completing one-time, individual transactions with government providers, but also better managing and self-governing one's personal and public affairs in order to make more informed choices that can partially tailor government service offerings as an integrative system. The risk with such models of self-empowerment is that they may impose new costs and demands on disadvantaged service users who have to acquire new skills in order to interact successfully with service delivery systems. Also, the growing enthusiasm for self-service, especially associated with e-delivery options, has the potential to marginalize the needs of those clients who need intensive personalized support.

Even across more mundane and routine transactional services, client-focused engagement and service personalization carries implications for how governments will maintain or alter the multiplicity of service delivery channels in the future. The United Kingdom transformational strategy highlighted earlier underscores service channel choice, for instance. Yet, over time, the value of such a range of offerings may erode or at least be challenged by the efficiency gains derived from incentives that augment online usage over other channels. Such a business case offers a potential nexus between customer and client considerations, and it is one that is consistent with the direction espoused by technology enthusiasts such as Bill Gates:

The ideal is to eventually eliminate the non-electronic ways of doing things by making sure that as you go into a service center somebody guides you through doing it in the automatic way or simply that you make it so simple, so pervasive that everybody is going to work that way (Gates 2006).

While the business case and the private interest of the world's largest operating systems and software company are self-evident, it is possible to make the link to the realm of citizen relations here if one believes that both economic and democratic prospects are increasingly likely to be interwoven with online venues and skill sets. At the broadest and most holistic level of democracy, the Internet has ushered in a plethora of hope and rhetoric for online engagement and renewal. Are there political benefits to be derived from a citizenry conducting its public services online, thereby being more likely to welcome online channels in democratic affairs?

There are complications. Cherney, for instance, asserts that the 'choice revolution' underpinning the expansion of information and the empowerment of individuals (perhaps at the nexus between customer and client dimensions to the preceding discussions) may also render democracy a mere choice among many, particularly for younger generations increasingly gravitating to online activity. While not necessarily negative in all respects, Cherney sees a precarious future for political engagement if democracy is left to compete in such a manner, framed as a 'mere' choice, and by extension, one framed more through the prism of customer than that of citizen, which carries with it some broader element of duty and responsibility (Cherney 2000).

Moreover, democracy remains a contested notion, even within jurisdictions committed to it, meaning that there is little consensus as to how electronic channels can or should be deployed to improve its performance. Shane contrasts the potential for democracy online across three well-established schools of thought, each implying a very different role for the public as well as elected officials and the manner by which each interacts and contributes to governance: election-centred, direct, and more deliberative models of democracy. Acknowledging electronic potential across all three, Shane concludes that any meaningful strategy for democratic renewal based partly on online capacities must encompass all three schools—just as our present institutional arrangements do currently albeit with mixed levels of success and emphasis across jurisdictions (Shane 2004).

In Canada, this type of transversal imposition of new technological capacities is not very far along due in large measure to the customer-centric flavour of e-government and service transformation. Although this characterization is somewhat looser federally—where some democratic experimentation has begun to appear—the emphasis of the past few years, as argued earlier, has been on a positively portrayed correlation of customer service and political trust (Heintzman and Marson 2005). Yet, much as this chapter has argued that there are multiple roles involving the public's interactions with governments, so too are there surely multiple forms of trust: a distinction that helps explain why, for example, the Government of Canada can score highly on service performance while suffering from eroding levels of political confidence and legitimacy.

Another challenging dimension of new democratic engagement opportunities involving online channels is the manner by which these opportunities involve more or less collaboration across different levels of government. As the customer logic fuels visions of a more seamless, monolithic public sector, the relational and policy aspects of both client and citizen relationships continue to rely more greatly on jurisdictional separation. This separation is important in not only placing boundaries around the highly complex transformations of specific service architectures of each government (i.e., the 311 strategies of cities, e-health prototypes provincially, and specific federal service streams such as tax filing, census completion, passport applications etc.), but also in clarifying the lines of political accountability between governments and their respective citizenries.

CHAPTER TWO

Are We Satisfied, and Is That the Point?[1]

Surveys of citizens' satisfaction with public services have become popular in recent decades. The rise of citizen surveys reflects several mega-trends in governance and administration, including neo-liberalism and new public management, and their appeal arguably stems from their apparent alignment with two dominant themes in contemporary public policy. The first is the emphasis on ensuring that public services reflect the needs and preferences of citizens rather than the internal priorities of administrative systems. This has been influenced by market-inspired models of the citizen as a 'customer' of government products and services (see chapter 1), and also takes impetus from the broader sense that citizens have grown increasingly unhappy with the performance of governments, leading to diminished engagement and trust (Bouckaert and Van de Walle 2003). The second theme is the increasing stress placed upon 'evidence' within policy formulation and public management (Nutley, Walter and Davies 2007). Proponents of evidence-based decision-making persuasively argue that managers require reliable and impartial data on policy and administrative problems to effectively navigate the complexities and constraints of the contemporary policy environment. Citizen satisfaction surveys are thus attractive because they promise simultaneously to enhance public input into government and the methodological rigour of the evidence used in official decision making.

Hence it is not surprising that citizen surveys have been embraced in many jurisdictions. Canada, a recognized leader in the field, has institutionalized a biennial survey series called Citizens First, which measures the extent to which Canadians are satisfied with a variety of government services. Canada has also produced the award-winning Common Measurements Tool (CMT), a standardized survey instrument designed for use in multiple jurisdictions to facilitate comparison of satisfaction levels between governments (Schmidt and Strickland 1998a; ICCS 2008a). Many practitioners and academic commentators believe these Canadian initiatives represent international best practice in satisfaction surveying, and the CMT has been adopted in numerous countries and translated into several languages (ICCS 2008b). This chapter will argue that even though the Canadian surveys deliberately use the terminology of 'citizen', they draw very heavily on private sector customer satisfaction survey methodologies.

While these research initiatives have informed and encouraged many innovations in government service delivery around the world, observers have also identified significant challenges in the implementation of contemporary service improvement and integration agendas (Dutil, Langford and Roy 2007; Langford 2008). These include bureaucratic resistance to the modernization and integration of services; dilemmas and trade-offs associated with responding to service users' demands in complex policy areas including health and social services; and ongoing resource limitations (Dutil, Langford and Roy 2007; Howard 2006; Langford 2008). Such obstacles are evident even in a success story like Canada, where commentators have noted the limited progress beyond streamlining of simple transactional services, an almost universal disinterest on the part of politicians, and an absence of meaningful citizen involvement in service improvement (Dutil, Langford and Roy 2007; Langford 2008).

There are many reasons for the mixed fortunes of contemporary Canadian service transformation agendas (Langford 2008). This chapter asks if the methodological choices involved in the design and implementation of Canada's Citizens First surveys might also present obstacles to the progress of service transformation in the country. To this end it reports the results of a systematic methodological review of the Citizens First surveys and Common Measurements Tool. The review is divided into two components. First, the chapter approaches Citizens First and the CMT from an epistemological perspective and asks whether the surveys generate valid knowledge of citizens' attitudes and preferences regarding public service delivery. This epistemological review reveals that the findings produced by Citizens First and the CMT are contestable from a number of different social research perspectives. Of course, whether or not the surveys are epistemologically sound, they can still influence administrative practices and the relationships between citizens and the state. The second part of the methodological review draws upon Law and Urry's (2004) suggestions that we need to pay attention to the ontological consequences of methodological choices and that we may critically interrogate methodologies on the basis of the 'realities' they help to produce. It suggests, consistent with chapter one of this book, that the Citizens First surveys have encouraged service delivery reforms that assume the service user is an informed customer seeking convenience and value from transactional government services.

As a result these reforms conflict with other important trends in governance and service delivery in Canada, and this dissonance must be overcome for further progress in service transformation to be achieved. These findings are timely and important because many countries are currently adopting or considering the Canadian methodology.

Background

Surveys of citizen satisfaction have been around in North American public services since the 1970s. They received a substantial boost in popularity and status in the early 1990s, when the publication of Osborne and Gaebler's *Reinventing Government* sparked a new interest in thinking of citizens as customers, and the administration of US President Clinton mandated the use of satisfaction surveys as part of the National Performance Review's "new customer service contract" with citizens (Osborne and Gaebler 1992; Pegnato 1997; Schachter 1995). This trend towards regarding citizens as customers has been associated with the new public management (Barzelay 1992; Hood 1991). In the literature on public sector reform, Canada is often regarded as a laggard or an exception to the new public management trend (Aucoin 2002).

Commentators note that successive Canadian governments have failed to articulate a positive reform agenda for public administration; politicians have not been involved in reforming bureaucracies in the same high profile way as in Australia, New Zealand, the United Kingdom and the United States, although they have been attracted by the downsizing and privatization elements of the new public management (Aucoin 2002; Bakvis 2000; Dwivedi and Gow 1999). Unlike the other Anglo-American jurisdictions, which embraced substantial public sector reform initiatives at the political level with positive visions of administrative transformation, Canada's notable reforms of the 1990s, both provincially and federally, were mostly negative exercises in reducing the size of government

(Clark 2002; Dwivedi and Gow 1999; Taras and Tupper 1994). Thus the government, led by then Prime Minister Jean Chrétien, initiated a drastic budget cutting exercise called Program Review in 1995 against a backdrop of substantial budget deficits. Although this initiative was successful in reducing deficits, it created problems for the federal government and public service. Research showed citizens to be deeply unhappy about cuts to services, while the federal bureaucracy was said to be experiencing poor morale, high levels of turnover and acute difficulty attracting new talent (Bourgault and Gusella 2001).

In the absence of a positive reform agenda at the political level, the task of revitalizing the Canadian public service in the late 1990s was left to the bureaucracy. Several renewal initiatives were developed within the senior levels of the federal service during this time (Ibid.). One of these was an effort by the Treasury Board Secretariat (the central agency responsible for overseeing budgeting, management and human resource practices in federal public service entities) to bring together officials across government to explore the 'service gap'—defined as the mismatch between the services citizens expect from governments and the services actually provided (CCMD 1999). As a result, the Citizen-Centred Service Network (CCSN) was created, composed of public servants from different jurisdictions and levels of government, as well as academics and consultants (Ibid.). The members of the CCSN accepted that in order to implement a successful "gap closure strategy", research was needed to discover the nature and extent of the service gap by exploring what citizens thought of specific services and their priorities for improvement (Bent, Kernaghan and Marson 1999).

This research agenda was shaped by a number of significant priorities and trends at the time. The issue of existing negative public attitudes to government was central (CCMD 1999). Network publications noted that citizen satisfaction surveys at that time were generally recording negative attitudes towards the public sector, especially when compared with the private sector (Bent, Kernaghan and Marson 1999). The CCSN asserted that this research was based on a number of problematic methodological assumptions and that more research was needed to clarify whether the public sector was performing as badly as suggested. The CCSN also emphasized the importance of exploring emerging models for reforming service delivery such as creating 'single windows' and developing telephone and Internet service channels. These efforts were motivated in part by the sense that dissatisfaction with specific services contributed to dissatisfaction with government in general, and that reversing perceptions of specific services was a necessary precursor to improving citizens' confidence and trust in government, despite mixed evidence concerning this linkage in the academic literature on citizen satisfaction (Bouckaert and Van de Walle 2003; Goodsell 1994).

The CCSN chose to develop citizen satisfaction surveys as its principal data collection instruments (CCMD 1999). The first survey, Citizens First, was undertaken in cooperation with a private sector management consulting firm, Erin Research Inc., in 1998 (Erin Research 1998). This survey found, contrary to some previous studies, that public attitudes to government services were not uniformly negative and that they often compared favourably with attitudes to private sector services (Ibid.). The analysis suggested that certain aspects of public service delivery—"timeliness", "knowledge", "competence", "courtesy and comfort", "fair treatment", and "outcome"—explained most of the variation in citizens' satisfaction with government services. These elements are referred to throughout the Citizens First reports as the '"drivers" of citizen satisfaction' (Ibid., 27–37).

Concurrently, Faye Schmidt, a private sector consultant working with the CCSN, developed the Common Measurements Tool as a DIY (do-it-yourself) survey that could be used by other jurisdictions to measure satisfaction in a manner similar to Citizens First (Schmidt and Strickland 1998a).[2] According to Schmidt, the "overriding consideration" in the design of the CMT survey instrument was that it was standardized to allow for benchmarking (hence 'Common Measurements') (Ibid., 19). The CMT includes a limited number of fields for qualitative responses. It is copyrighted, and organizations that use the tool must comply with licensing conditions (ICCS 2008b). For jurisdictions outside of Canada and private sector users, this includes a fee payable to the Institute for Citizen-Centred Service (ICCS), a non-profit entity created in 2001 that has responsibility for the ongoing development and marketing of the CMT. The ICCS notes that many jurisdictions have taken up the CMT; thirty-nine countries have purchased licences, it has been translated into several languages, and some governments have used it to develop their own versions of Citizens First, as exemplified by New Zealand's Kiwis Count initiative (ICCS 2008c).

These survey instruments were designed to be used by public managers. The CMT comes with its own Manager's Guide (Schmidt and Strickland 1998b). The language of this document targets those officials caught between "increasing demands for services and ongoing funding limitations" (Ibid., 3). Among the claimed benefits to "your organization" are an ability to provide feedback to staff and political leaders about program effectiveness, and to "validate requests for increased resources to areas in need of improvement" (Ibid., 6). The CMT gives examples of satisfaction data being used by officials to "effectively support funding requests" (Ibid., 8). In cases where public managers cannot secure enough funds to satisfy citizens' demands, "the information collected [through the CMT] will assist organizations to target service areas where a communications strategy is needed in order to manage [service users'] expectations" (Ibid., 3). The Citizens First series is also aimed at a managerial audience. As a result, some of the survey findings are downplayed because they are beyond the scope of managers' control. For example, although the 1998 Citizens First study finds that general attitudes towards government are also drivers of satisfaction with services, since "citizens who believe that governments do an excellent job rate service quality higher than those who do not" (Erin Research 1998: 34), the survey justifies leaving this off the list of drivers in part because managers cannot control this variable:

> Should this attitude be included as a driver of service quality? Logically, it very well could, but practically, it may not be useful to do so. The five original drivers are all part of the service delivery fabric. They are completely or at least partially within the control of service providers. If there is a problem with one of the five, steps can be taken by governments to improve service. But a citizen's belief that government does a good or poor job is beyond the immediate control of service providers ... As a matter of strategy, it seems better to restrict the idea of drivers to matters that can be changed and refined (Ibid., 35).

This quote highlights the deliberate restriction of the discussion to those aspects that are within the responsibility of 'service providers', as distinct from those drivers that are under the control of citizens and their representatives, such as public attitudes towards government policies.

In summary, Canada's focus on satisfaction surveys emerged in a context of political disinterest in administrative renewal combined with substantial retrenchment of public services and public discontent about government. The surveys were initiated by a network of senior officials who assumed responsibility for revitalizing the public service, and who sought to empower public managers with new tools and evidence to support and validate decisions and requests.

Citizen surveys as knowledge creation

Given that Citizens First and the Common Measurements Tool utilize the language of social science and claim to provide compelling evidence about citizens' preferences and priorities, it is appropriate to ask whether their methodologies meet the standards of knowledge creation in social research. Of course, there is no consensus on the criteria for making valid knowledge claims in the social sciences. Different methodological traditions have their own views on the base conditions that must be met for credible evidence to be generated. Survey researchers, for instance, tend to adopt positivist assumptions and defer to the conventions concerning confidence and validity associated with statistical traditions (Fowler 2002; Woock 1981. This section holds Citizens First and the CMT up against these methodological principles to see if they comply with the conventions accepted within the academic surveying community. It also draws on the hermeneutic or interpretive paradigm (Bevir, Rhodes and Weller 2003; Dryzek 1982) in order to highlight additional potential points of epistemological critique in Citizens First and the CMT. The epistemological review is divided into three themes: representativeness; causality; and subjectivity. This section also points out how these methodological challenges are linked to the managerial origins of service transformation in Canada.

Representativeness

The Citizens First surveys are based on random samples of Canadian households in order to permit their findings to be generalized to the population.[3] However, this does not guarantee that the findings are representative of the population. A significant challenge in survey administration is the tendency of some members of the sample not to complete the survey; much research has documented the general decline in survey response rates over the 20th century (Fowler 2002). For example, the 1998 Citizens First survey was distributed to 34,900 households and 2,900 complete responses were received (Erin Research 1998). Erin Research Inc. calculates the 'return rate' as 9.2 percent, and notes that this is "a high return rate for a mail survey distributed by a private firm" (Ibid., 3).

The response rates for the subsequent surveys were as follows: Citizens First 2000, 9 percent (Erin Research 2000); Citizens First 3, 14.3 percent (Erin Research 2003); Citizens First 4, 13.4 percent (Phase 5 Consulting Group 2005); and Citizens First 5, 13 percent (Erin Research 2008). Non-response is typically non-random, meaning that some individuals in the sample are more likely to respond than others. This means that even though the composition of individuals in a random sample may closely reflect the population, the responders are usually systematically different from the population (Fowler 2002). Other things being equal, the lower the response rate, the more unrepresentative the responders will be, and the greater the error in the survey results. Although there is no universally accepted minimum response rate in survey research, there are general standards for survey response in both academia and public policy. For instance, the US Office of Management and Budget requires surveys performed by external contractors to have response rates above 75 percent (Ibid.). Fowler suggests that response rates below 20 percent in surveys do not produce valid estimates:

> …one will occasionally see reports of mail surveys in which 5% to 20% of the selected sample responded. In such instances, the final sample has little relationship to the original sampling process; those responding are essentially self-selected. It is very unlikely that such procedures will provide any credible statistics about the characteristics of the population as a whole (Ibid., 42).

Fowler provides a demonstration of the effect that non-response has on the confidence one can place in a survey estimate. Table 1 is an adaptation of his explanation. It shows that if 50 percent of the respondents answer yes to a 'yes/no' question, and the response rate is 10 percent, then the true population proportion answering yes could range between 5 percent and 95 percent, meaning the reader can have virtually no confidence that the statistic is an accurate estimate of the true population proportion. This suggests that the figures reported in the Citizens First studies do not match with the true population values by a wide margin.

Table 1: Effect of response rates on range of possible true percentages

	When the response rate is				
	90%	70%	50%	30%	10%
If 50% respond "Yes" to a "Yes/No" question, the true number answering "Yes" could range from:	34-55%	35-65%	25-75%	15-85%	5-95%

Source: Adapted from *Survey Research Methods*, 3rd edition, 2002 by F. J. Fowler, page 45.

Research has identified the population subgroups that are more likely to respond to mail surveys. This can help to predict the directions in which the Citizens First research might be biased due to non-response. Fowler argues that people who are more interested in the subject matter are more likely to respond, and "[t]his means that mail surveys with low response rates may be biased significantly in ways that are related directly to the purposes of the research" (Ibid.). Those who wish to support the underdog are also more likely to return surveys, which is relevant in Citizens First as individuals may have responded to defend public services against the prevailing criticism, leading to inflated positive evaluations of services. Similarly, Van Goor and Stuiver (1998) review research on non-response and suggest that responders are more likely than non-responders to find the topic of the survey salient to their lives; to be directly involved in the subject matter of the survey; to vote; and to have strong and favourable opinions concerning the survey items. Finally, non-response is associated with language differences, literacy problems, physical and mental incapacity, and lack of a fixed address, which could be dimensions along which satisfaction varies (Fowler 2002).

Among other things, these points suggest that the responders to Citizens First probably have more favourable attitudes to government service delivery than the general Canadian population. Unfortunately, the authors of the Citizens First studies do not acknowledge in their reports that such low response rates are a serious problem. On the contrary, they suggest the response rates are high in comparison to similar private sector surveys, and misleadingly assert that, because each survey attracted thousands of respondents, the findings are necessarily representative of the Canadian population (Erin Research 2008). At the same time, they also attempt to correct for non-response bias by reweighting the sample for known population proportions of age, gender and region. Yet as Van Goor and Stuiver observe, "in practical research, precisely because information on the dependent variables is lacking for the nonresponders, weighting does not solve the problem of nonresponse bias. Evidently, the only real solution to the problem of nonresponse bias is still to increase response as much as possible" (Van Goor and Stuiver 1998: 497).

Causality

The Citizens First reports make several explicit and implicit causal claims about the conditions that lead to increased citizen satisfaction with government services. The strongest and most consistent claims are made in relation to the so called 'drivers' of citizen satisfaction, where it is suggested that achieving consistently high satisfaction ratings in relation to specific aspects of service delivery will directly increase overall satisfaction with government service delivery. This set of causal claims relies on regression analysis of the survey data. In addition, starting with Citizens First 3, the researchers employ structural equation modeling (SEM) to support a claim that satisfaction with specific aspects of service delivery leads to increased trust in government (Erin Research 2003).

Regression and SEM are designed for exploring associations between variables in data. Regression's key function is to allow the researcher to control for the impact of known 'background variables' in order to isolate relationships between variables of interest (Miles and Shelvin 2001). SEM is essentially a more sophisticated form of regression analysis that allows for non-linearity and testing of sets of relationships between multiple variables simultaneously (Biddle and Marlin 1987). Most statisticians would agree regression and SEM cannot in and of themselves definitively prove the existence of causal relationships in the real world because, strictly speaking, the ability to infer causality is a function of the way in which data is collected, not the analysis. Yet both forms of analysis are used regularly in social research to look for the existence of causal relationships and to see if the data supports or disconfirms certain causal hypotheses.

There is some consensus on what is required for these sorts of cautious causal inferences to be made using regression and SEM (McCoach, Black and O'Connell 2007; Miles and Shelvin 2001). This includes: (1) isolation of the variables of interest from the effects of all relevant background variables; (2) strong associations between variables of interest; (3) the temporal precedence of the independent variables over the dependent variables; and (4) a plausible theory that supports the causal hypotheses and the absence of plausible theories suggesting causality in other directions. Citizens First does not achieve temporal precedence because the data on satisfaction are all collected simultaneously, so the data cannot rule out the plausible alternative hypothesis that respondents established their satisfaction levels on the dependent variable—overall satisfaction with government services and trust in government—before or at the same time as the independent variable—specific aspects of a service experience. The causal claims in Citizens First may well be true, but their validity cannot be ascertained in the absence of more appropriate data, such as those generated through longitudinal and/or experimental research designs.

In spite of these limitations, the language used in the Citizens First reports is strongly and confidently causal. The authors not only assert that they have found statistical evidence for causal relationships, but they go further and present these relationships as certain and invariable—as if the independent variables will always cause the predicted effects on the dependent variables. For instance, the original Citizens First report stresses the causal power of the drivers:

> ...there is a strong linear relationship between the number of drivers scoring good and service quality. This result is extremely well grounded. It is based on responses of 2,900 Canadians to an enormous range of services at three levels of government. The generality of the finding cannot be questioned. It is important to emphasize the soundness of the result because of its far-reaching implications: *If governments provide an acceptable level of service – 4 or 5 out of 5 – on these five drivers, they will achieve service quality ratings of 85 out of 100* (Erin Research 1998: 32, emphasis original).

The certainty of the causal mechanisms is emphasized more strongly in Citizens First 2000, which asserts that "[p]roviding good service on each dimension guarantees high quality service ratings from citizens" (Erin Research 2000: 39). In relation to the SEM analysis of the impact of drivers on citizens' trust in government, Citizens First 3 is unambiguous about causality and the confidence that should be placed in the modeling:

> Does the connection also run the other way? Do individuals with high confidence in government perceive public services as better than those with less confidence? In fact, the link goes mainly in one direction. Good service creates a positive view of government, but citizens' overall confidence in government has a barely measurable impact on their ratings of individual government services...Satisfaction with government services contributes powerfully to citizens' confidence in government. The quantitative model...is proof of this (Erin Research 2003: 15, 21).[4]

The Citizens First reports also make recommendations on matters that are not covered in the survey data. At the end of the 1998 Citizens First report, in a chapter entitled "The Path Forward", the authors suggest that the "[r]esults of Citizens First point to the seven goal areas", which include specific initiatives like creating intergovernmental teams to champion service transformation; forming new public-private partnerships; promoting single-window initiatives; and developing new accountability, monitoring and reward structures based on the service delivery performance of individual staff members. The report claims that these recommendations "are specific and far reaching. They are grounded in the experience of a representative cross-section of Canadians with all three levels of government in each province and territory" (Erin Research 1998: 83). The suggestion is that the research found these strategies to be effective ways of increasing citizen satisfaction with services. In reality, however, most of these recommended strategies and implied causal relationships were not directly explored or tested in the survey. They represent complex administrative reforms that are beyond the scope of citizen satisfaction surveys. Studies that investigate such reforms and their impacts tend to use interpretive, historical and case-study methods that are better able to take into account the specific institutional circumstances in which these kinds of initiatives are enacted and the multiple interests and trade-offs involved (Bevir, Rhodes and Weller 2003; Dutil, Langford and Roy 2007).

Subjectivity

In the literature on citizen satisfaction with public services, measures of satisfaction are typically regarded as 'soft' or 'subjective' indicators of service quality, as opposed to 'hard' or 'objective' measures such as data on administrative inputs and outputs (Kampen 2007; Kelly and Swindell 2002; Parks 1984; Van Ryzin and Immerwahr 2007). There is a lively debate in the literature about how seriously satisfaction measures should be taken, with some arguing that they are an inaccurate way to measure the performance of government services, since many citizens do not have the expertise, information and time needed to evaluate government programs, leading to errors of 'assessment' and 'attribution' (Kelly and Swindell 2002; Parks 1984; Stipak 1979; Swiss 1992). In contrast, others defend subjective measures of satisfaction on the grounds that in a democracy, citizen evaluations of public services are "important in and of themselves", since citizens are the ultimate beneficiaries of government services (Fitzgerald and Durant 1980; Stipak 1979). The Citizens First and CMT surveys invoke just such a democratic justification: survey results are presented as a "powerful citizens' mandate to improve the quality of government services" (Erin Research 2000: 16).

The debate between objective and subjective measurements reminds us that subjective indicators raise complex issues around validity. The difficulty is that "[t]here is no external criterion" for figuring out whether satisfaction levels reported in surveys reflect true underlying subjective states (Fowler 2002: 100). One suggested approach for improving validity in subjective measures is to try to get at the same subjective state in different ways, such as through different questions. Then "patterns of association among questions" can be studied to determine if consistent responses are received (Ibid., 101–102). The Citizens First series of studies measures satisfaction with government services in different ways by asking about satisfaction with public services in general and also with specific services. It finds a pattern similar to other studies, in that questions about satisfaction with government and public services in general elicit more negative responses than questions about specific services, especially those recently experienced.

The authors of the Citizens First reports interpret this to mean that measures of satisfaction with specific services are more valid than measures of services in general. In the first report they argue that "[t]he [attitude to services in general] is essentially a stereotype, a distillation of reality that selects from the experiences that gave rise to it" (Erin Research 1998: 7). By contrast, perceptions of recent and specific experiences should be given greater credence since they "draw on particular memories and actual experiences" (Ibid.). Citizens First 2000 argues that asking citizens in surveys about their attitudes to government services in general encourages them to regurgitate "myths and stereotypes" that are supported by "information (and misinformation) that people pick up from media accounts and conversations with friends" (Erin Research 2000: 14). In Citizens First 3, new terminology is introduced to capture this distinction; questions about service in general are said to measure "service reputation", while questions about specific encounters measure "service experience" (Erin Research 2003: 11). Citizens First 4 cements the idea:

> Similar to Citizens First 1, the latest version of Citizens First shows that the service quality reputation of governments are [sic] not consistent with ratings provided on actual experiences with government. As noted in 1998, when rating government services in general, citizens may draw on a range of opinions, experiences and reference group influences that tend to be more negative. The myth that all, or even many, public services are poor quality still persists. Yet when one gets past the mythical rhetoric and anecdotal examples of poor experiences, many government services rate rather well (Phase 5 Consulting Group 2005: 13).

The clear and consistent implication is that measures of specific interactions are based on real events and experiences authentic to the respondent, whereas measures of satisfaction in general are influenced by vague sentiments and stereotypes. Thus, while the authors of Citizens First align themselves with those who think subjective measures are important and valid, they also believe that some subjective measures are more important and valid than others.

This approach of selectively dismissing some subjective attitudes while embracing others is problematic for at least two reasons. First, it fails to acknowledge that general indicators capture attitudes and opinions that are not solicited in questions about specific services. Bouckaert and Van de Walle (2003) note that when citizens evaluate government service in general, they tend to consider a wider range of factors, including underlying policy frameworks, recent political events, and ideological elements. These factors are highly relevant to government service delivery. Pegnato (1997) makes the point that *citizens* are not just *customers* who receive of government services, but also *owners* who make evaluations of the performance of governments as a whole and can force a top-down change in government policies and services through elections. Hence their opinions on the general performance of government are highly relevant to the direction of public policy and service delivery.

The second major problem with this dismissal of opinions about overall government service delivery performance is that it assumes that citizens are unable to think critically for themselves. It is a stark rejection of the basic hermeneutic assumption that individuals actively and creatively interpret their worlds and attach meaning to the events around them (Bevir, Rhodes and Weller 2003; Dryzek 1982). From the hermeneutic perspective, one can ask, what authority do the authors of Citizens First have to suggest that some responses reflect the actual opinions of the survey respondents, while others do not? This dismissal of certain attitudes, coupled with the highly deterministic claims about the drivers, creates a picture of citizens as essentially passive receptacles whose subjective states are determined by external stimuli at two levels. Their attitudes toward services in general are not internally generated, but are the product of deceptive 'myths and stereotypes'. At the same time, their attitudes to specific services are assumed to be externally determined by the nature of the service delivery process, since good performance on the drivers allegedly always leads to high levels of satisfaction. Ironically, an approach that justifies itself with an appeal to democratic principles ultimately dis-empowers citizens by presenting their subjective states as externally determined by a combination of prevailing ideologies (in the case of general attitudes) and objective features of the service interaction (in the case of specific experiences).

An ontological critique of citizen satisfaction

For some social scientists, the only legitimate mode of academic critique is that which is targeted at the validity of knowledge claims, not the political assumptions, motivations and consequences of the research (Hammersley 2005). According to this view, methodologies should only be judged on their suitability for generating valid knowledge about the world. The assumption, of course, is that there is a world that exists independently of social science and that researchers can come to discover it by applying the right kinds of empirical methods. There are many who reject this line of reasoning.

Here we focus on the work of John Law and John Urry, who are critical of the 'epistemological' approach to evaluating methodological choices. For Law and Urry the implementation of social science methodologies always has the effect of "enacting" realities into being. Instead of viewing the social sciences as revealing a pre-given reality, they suggest that social research is in an interactive relationship with the world, whereby it both uncovers the existence of realities and at the same time "brings into being what it discovers" (Law and Urry 2004: 393). Hence their focus is ontological—on the effects of methodological choices on reality. It is also political, since it suggests that methodological choices can enact, perpetuate or undermine particular institutional arrangements. This is not to say that Law and Urry believe social scientists can bring whatever realities into being they choose simply by conducting research. The effects of social research are unpredictable; hence, studies seeking to establish the ontological impacts of methodological choices should only make contingent and tentative claims about cause and effect. In addition to rejecting the view that reality exists separately from social science, Law and Urry also argue against the prevailing idea that there is a single reality or 'world' (Ibid., 396). They claim that if different methodologies can bring different worlds into being, then the implementation of these methodologies will lead to multiple worlds that overlap and interact with each other. In the case of this research project, Law and Urry's work leads us to ask, what kinds of realities are enacted through the methodological choices in satisfaction surveys? Furthermore, how do these realities overlap and interact with other realities?

Law and Urry's post-structuralist focus on the politics of knowledge and the productive nature of social science can be linked to citizen satisfaction through the work of Chris Weedon (1997), who develops Foucault's notion of the 'discursive field'. This concept assumes that language, which is organized in the form of discourses, structures the possible identities that individuals can legitimately assume in a given context, and fundamentally affects the prevailing institutional arrangements and power hierarchies. In this approach, individual identities and subjectivities (emotional states) do not exist prior to discourse and language. Rather, language provides the preconditions for individual identities and for the emotions and interpretations that individuals feel. There are usually several discourses in a discursive field and these typically exist within a hierarchy, meaning that some discourses are dominant and others are subordinate (Weedon 1997). Linking the concepts of ontological politics and discursive field together, we might say that methodological choices occur within discursive fields where dominant discourses have a determining role in shaping the possibilities for analytical action, but these discursive fields in turn are also impacted by the methodological choices that are made by the actors. Hence there is an iterative relationship between social research and the discursive fields in which it operates.

In Canada, *government service transformation* is the relevant discursive field, and *citizen-centred service* is the dominant discourse within the field. The dominant discourse is made up of many elements, including the languages, practices, and knowledge utilized in and produced through satisfaction surveys. The discourse constructs and makes available several identities for the users of government services. These include the *customer* or *client*, who is understood as a demanding, opinionated service recipient with a sense of their own needs and priorities but who, nevertheless, has the same service delivery preferences as the majority of the population. This sameness is established through the reporting of survey data on the drivers of satisfaction, which allegedly shows that, in spite of minor variations between subgroups of service users, all citizens want similar things from their service deliverers (see the previous section).

The discourse organizes the subjectivities of customers in terms of degrees of satisfaction. Subjectivities of satisfaction are produced in a linear, ordinal and quantitative fashion through the use of Likert scales in surveys and bar charts in reports. In the process of establishing the customer the discourse creates the identity of the minority individual whose special needs must be considered, while simultaneously subordinating these needs by asserting the overwhelming constancy of typical customers' preferences. A further identity is the 'taxpayer', who has an indirect interest in service delivery, since they may be contributing resources to fund services. By establishing the strength and consistency of mainstream service preferences, subordinating special needs, and incorporating the interests of the taxpayer, the treatment of subject positions within the Canadian discourse of citizen-centred service draws upon and reinforces the broader contemporary neo-liberal discourse that characterizes particular types of service users, including vulnerable individuals dependent on social programs as "special interests" and "deviants" (Denis 1995; Dobrowolsky 1998).

The citizen-centred service discourse also establishes a series of identities for public officials. It draws upon the influential discourses of public choice; managerialism; total quality management; and customer service (du Gay 2000; Dutil, Langford and Roy 2007) to construct a caricatured model of the traditional bureaucrat, who regards citizens as a nuisance and avoids efforts to improve service delivery (du Gay 2000; Kettl 1993). This bureaucrat is subordinated to the entrepreneurial, responsive, customer-focused public manager who is a champion of citizen-centred service. The champion identity is constructed as pivotal to the success of service transformation, and requires autonomy from above and below. Above the champions are politicians, who, in an era of fiscal retrenchment and privatization, must be persuaded to make the improvement of public services a priority. They cannot be relied upon to initiate reform on their own, and are potential sources of resistance to managerial initiative—though they can also supply financial and political support. Below the champions are front-line staff, who must be motivated and supported by the champions to see value in their work and overcome a culture of unresponsiveness.

The citizen-centred service discourse draws upon citizen satisfaction surveys to legitimize a new set of institutional arrangements for public service delivery. The institutional centrepiece is the single-window or one-stop-shop that brings together multiple services in one location in a consistent format. Australia's Centrelink and Service Canada are examples of this model (Flumian, Coe and Kernaghan 2007). Where additional 'channels' of service are provided (such as telephone and Internet) strong emphasis is placed on ensuring consistency across the different channels. The Citizens First surveys support this integration through their demonstration of the consistency of the drivers of satisfaction across service delivery areas. The dominant discourse constructs and criticizes a contrasting set of institutional arrangements for service delivery, which are based on functionally differentiated 'stovepipes' or 'silos' that each offer a limited range of services requiring citizens to move between different organizations to get what they require from government. The stovepipe model is dismissed as inconvenient for the customer and inefficient because it involves duplication.

There are three critical problems with the realities that are enacted by the Canadian citizen satisfaction research and its associated discourse of citizen-centred service. The first concerns the attempt to impose the customer identity at the expense of alternatives (Dutil, Langford and Roy 2007). As a number of critics of the customer service agenda have noted, the importation of customer service techniques and philosophies into the public sector belies the fact that it is often very difficult to determine who the customer of a public service is and what they want (Kettl 1993; Swiss 1992). Furthermore, there are certain administrative contexts—such as industrial regulation, criminal justice and human services—where it is inappropriate to talk about customers because the function of administrators is not to strive to give users everything they want (Pegnato 1997; Swiss 1992). Citizens First and the CMT make this error by referring to subjects of regulatory agencies as customers. Another point is that the standardized customer model conflicts with the growing interest, especially within human and social services, in 'individualized service delivery' and in enhancing the voice of each client in the service interaction (Yeatman, Dowsett and Guransky 2009). The customer model represents a production line approach, while the individualized model demands considerable freedom and discretion for staff to operate in an open-ended fashion (Ibid.; Dutil, Langford and Roy 2007; Swiss 1992).

A more general point is that public service delivery, especially in complex fields such as the human services, is rife with tensions and dilemmas. According to Hoggett and others (2007) administrators working in these domains require a capacity for dealing with contradictions; firm values; and a sense of authority beyond responding to the immediate wishes of the client in order to operate effectively in 'dilemmatic space'. The recommendations supplied by Citizens First do not offer guidance on how to reconcile tensions between drivers of satisfaction, or how to deal with more substantive trade-offs and contradictions in policies. It is not surprising that Canadians reformers—along with practitioners in other countries that draw on the same customer-service oriented discourses of citizen satisfaction—have struggled to incorporate more complex services into their transformation agendas, and that competing reform discourses such as decentralization, outsourcing and specialization have to date been equally or more influential (Dutil, Langford and Roy 2007).

Another concern with the realities created by the service satisfaction movement is the narrow and passive role envisaged for citizens within service transformation. Schachter's critique of the customer service orientation under Clinton and Gore in the United States captures this idea:

Reinventing government centers on how public administrators can satisfy their customers. Administrators are the actors; they survey client attitudes, make services convenient, empower their subordinates, and decide which programs to contract out or decentralize-in many ways acting as owners do in private business. Reform means change in administrative work routines, bureaucratic cultures, and agency procedures to allow various departments to develop entrepreneurs and leaders. Because members of the public are only the recipients of administrative action, little thought is directed to changing their routines to increase the probability that leaders will emerge from their ranks. The assumption is that changing bureaucratic structures and relationships will yield a more sensitive and responsive public service (Schachter 1995: 534).

This suggests that a reform ostensibly designed to shift the focus from internal to external drivers of performance actually does the opposite, by introducing a new emphasis on the role that managers must play in promoting change. Citizen input is limited to providing feedback on the existing suite of programs and services, and there is little interest in encouraging and enabling citizens to become more informed and take greater responsibility for designing programs and services. In contrast to Schachter, the ontological analysis presented in this chapter suggests that customer service reform movements do actually encourage change in citizens. As we have seen, citizen satisfaction movements promote changes in the identities and subjectivities that recipients of public services adopt and experience. Citizens undergo transformation in this process, and the new subjectivities and institutions allow for a narrow range of input and do not permit citizens to have a say in the underlying structure and format of program design and delivery. Despite the questionable claims in Citizens First about the positive impact the customer service model of government is having on levels of engagement, trust and efficacy, it remains to be seen whether the model will facilitate citizen involvement. In an age of heightened individualization, social activism and value pluralism, it is easy to imagine citizens finding this model of participation wanting.

As this book describes, the third area of concern relates to the organizational realities surrounding service delivery. The Canadian satisfaction surveys have been interpreted as providing justification for greater centralization in service delivery, in both horizontal (inter-departmental) and vertical (inter-jurisdictional) terms. Furthermore, there is also a clear desire to promote the retention of service delivery within government rather than contracting out delivery functions to private providers. This directly contradicts several competing discourses and interests in contemporary service delivery. In some Canadian jurisdictions attempts to integrate service delivery functions into a single window have been impeded by the legacy of 1990s decentralization and outsourcing campaigns, which created a new group of stakeholders with vested interests in a disaggregated model of service provision. Furthermore, there is the non-trivial politics of branding associated with service integration. Public organizations and their political masters are generally keen to take credit for the programs and services they fund, whereas the single window model tends to hide the originators of the service behind the generic service agency's brand. This politics of branding can be especially acute where service integration is attempted between levels of government in a federation (Bakvis and Juillet 2004). Underlying this is a more worrying issue of attribution and accountability. Concealing the originators of programs and services behind the elegant simplicity of 'single windows' arguably makes it more difficult for citizens to know who to hold accountable for inadequacies and failures in service provision. Given these challenges, it is not surprising that while the single-window model dominates discussions of service transformation in Canada, the true extent of service integration has been limited.

Conclusion

Citizens First and the CMT have not been subjected to critical scrutiny in the decade since they were introduced. This is surprising given the role these research agendas have played in shaping the discursive field of service transformation in Canada and elsewhere. It is important to acknowledge this contribution and recognize that the surveys have provided a new means for citizens to exercise input, new sources of legitimacy for service deliverers, and new tools for managers designing programs and services.

This chapter sought to understand the role of methodology in explaining why the Canadian service transformation agenda has encountered significant obstacles. It highlights the complexities surrounding citizen satisfaction surveys, both in terms of the technical considerations associated with making knowledge claims, and the intended and unintended impacts of social research on the world. In the name of creating a simple but compelling story for managers, the authors of Citizens First have evaded important epistemological concerns about representativeness, causality and subjectivity. Furthermore,

Citizens First and the CMT have propelled the customer service and single window discourses to the centre of service transformation rhetoric. These approaches are at odds with other aspects of contemporary administration and governance. There is a risk that they will crowd out alternative ways of thinking about and organizing service delivery and citizen engagement.

This chapter demonstrates the complex interactions between methodological choices in citizen satisfaction surveys and the realities of service transformation in Canada. An understanding of these interactions is necessary in order to develop more effective strategies for meaningfully engaging citizens in the service delivery process.

Endnotes

[1] A version of this chapter was originally published in the *International Review of Administrative Sciences*, Vol. 76, No. 1, March 2010.

[2] Although it appears that the CMT is similar to the survey instrument used in the Citizens First surveys, direct comparisons are hampered by the fact that the instruments used in the Citizens First surveys are not publically available. The author sent a request to the Institute for Citizen-Centred Service (ICCS) in 2008 seeking access to the Citizens First instruments, but the request was turned down.

[3] Citizens First and Citizens First 2000 were mail surveys. One-sixth of the responses in Citizens First 3 came from an online survey, with the rest coming from a mail survey. Citizens First 4 used mail surveys only, while half of the Citizens First 5 responses were from an online survey, and the other half were from mail (Erin Research 2008). Each iteration of Citizens First was made up of separate surveys conducted in each Canadian jurisdiction by participating organizations. These separate surveys were then weighted to ensure correspondence to known population proportions. The authors stress that the "procedures followed in fielding the survey were very similar" across the five Citizens First studies (Ibid., 97).

[4] Citizens First 5 adopts a more measured tone about the causal power of the drivers, noting that "[o]ne can never be absolutely certain what the drivers are in a given situation without doing primary research" (Erin Research 2008: 70). The report notes that there are often "structural reasons" for the differences in satisfaction scores between different public organizations, making it imperative to "compare apples with apples." That being said, the general predictive validity of the drivers continues to be asserted: "[f]or those who cannot do their own customer research…one cannot go far wrong with the driver model…It is a reliable framework for action" (Ibid.).

CHAPTER THREE

Can We Create
a Service Culture?

In the Government of Canada, the earliest, most eloquent cry for improved services was made by the highest ranking executive in the bureaucracy, the Clerk of the Privy Council in the late 1980s. Paul Tellier even made improving services to the citizenry a cornerstone to the famous PS 2000 vision (Kernaghan 1991; Rawson 1991) that was designed to establish a public service for the 21st century. Critical to PS 2000, and to the likes of Osborne and Gaebler's *Reinventing Government*, was a conviction that the 'culture' of the public service had to change in order to measurably improve public services from one that was inward-looking to one that was more focused on the needs of Canadians (Osborne and Gaebler 1992; Seidle 1995). A generation later, while governments across Canada have done a great deal to improve service to the public, the objective of creating a genuine 'service culture' seems as difficult as ever to realize.

Research and practices in the private sector have pointed to a solution in terms of understanding 'culture' and the best ways of shaping it so that it could in turn make service companies more competitive. Since the early 1990s, it has been known as the 'satisfaction mirror'—an axiom that employees who were happy in their jobs were more likely to deliver better service than employees who were not. "Service-driven service companies" were found to thrive on a "service profit chain"—a model that placed employee satisfaction as a critical link between internal service quality and customer satisfaction/retention and profit (Schlesinger and Heskett 1991a, b). Some public administration scholars in Canada were also attentive to the phenomena. *Canadian Public Administration*, the flagship journal of public administration in the country, published an article on the critical link between employee engagement and customer satisfaction based on a case study performed at Xerox (Lacasse 1991) as a part of a trend of scholarly material (Roth, Bozinoff and MacIntosh 1990; Séguin 1991; Lacasse 1991; Bouchard 1991; Marson 1991; Morin 1992; Das and McKenzie 1995). Further studies in the private sector showed that employee commitment translated as better service, and ultimately made a company more profitable in addition to being competitive (Rucci, Kirk and Quinn 1998).

This chapter argues that while a 'service culture' can be promoted in the public sector, its impact will be limited by a number of factors that invariably impair the construct of a genuine public service 'value chain'. First, the current *nature of the work* makes the improvement of a service culture inherently difficult. Front-line employees in the public service have relatively little discretion in serving clients and must follow procedures established to ensure fairness of service. The service culture of the public service, inevitably, has had to conform to bureaucratic rules, strictures and rigours. Second, the *nature of the service* itself is limiting. Most government services are 'low involvement'—the relationship may be life-long, but infrequent, routine, and in little need of the personalization typical of a 'service culture'. A service culture in bureaucratic terms is not likely to go beyond the courteous, timely and effective delivery of prescribed solutions. Third, it is difficult to maintain a service culture where the clients have no incentive to seek the service except to avoid an outlaw existence. It cannot be forgotten that most citizens do not typically require an active service from government—it is demanded by the state or its provision is imposed by a state monopoly. Fourth, evidence collected by governments shows that public servants are largely satisfied with their work, and that the service culture is already healthy (albeit within its limits). This may be promising in some regards, but it also carries a risk; satisfied workers may not necessarily be willing to change their customer-relations practices radically without substantial incentives. Finally, the efforts required to achieve an 'engaged' workforce can be expensive and subject to laws of diminishing returns. Governments are already loath to subject their services to genuine cost-effectiveness comparisons. Indeed, without this vital, missing element, it will be difficult to argue that there is anything more than a superficial public value chain.

It took more than a decade for the public service to react to what was published in *Canadian Public Administration* in the early 1990s in terms of exploring the link between a healthy working culture and the concept of employee satisfaction. In 2003 the British Columbia Auditor-General

(BCA-G) argued that "research has shown there is a relationship between employee engagement, good organizational performance, and customer satisfaction" (British Columbia 2002–03: 2). A few years later, two executives in the Government of Canada argued that the private sector's "service profit chain" could be applied to government service (Heintzman and Marson 2005). The "public sector service value chain" predicted that customer satisfaction would rise if front-line service providers were also 'satisfied'. They went further by maintaining that increases in customer satisfaction would lead to "confidence in the public service" and "confidence in government" (Ibid.). It followed, therefore, that governments had to address issues around employee satisfaction and commitment. "By applying the same continuous, targeted improvement approach to the drivers of employee engagement satisfaction/commitment," they stated, "public sector managers may well be able to make gains in this area [service satisfaction] as well" (Ibid., 569).

The ambitions and the possibilities are irreconcilable. It will be difficult to create a genuine service culture if public servants are called to deliver impersonal services. The only way to genuinely change the service culture will be to rethink the policies and procedures around the services themselves, and to develop genuinely value-added products that are likely to attract a clientele, instead of citizens wishing merely to live within the boundaries of the law. On this front, governments have done little. While the work of ensuring courteous, efficient and knowledgeable service cannot end, the objective of developing a genuine 'service culture' based on 'cultured services' (i.e., services that genuinely attract customers and clienteles by their customization) will be challenging at best and most likely elusive.

Towards an index: employee 'satisfaction', 'commitment' and 'engagement'

The public value equation holds that satisfied customers of government services are more likely to have been greeted and served by satisfied employees. Until recently, attention focused on the job satisfaction of front-line public service employees was relatively rare and mostly an academic pursuit. In his classic *Street-Level Bureaucracy* (1980), Michael Lipsky argued that in order to draw satisfaction from their work, employees "routinized", "controlled clients" and used "coping mechanisms". Lipsky argued that workload was a critical factor, as were the nature of the clients themselves, many of whom were "weak" and "endlessly demanding". He noted that there could be a significant job frustration, and indeed "sabotage" of the work expected, if conditions deteriorated beyond the control of the service delivery officer.

In their study of front-line workers in the American mid-west and south-west, Maynard-Moody and Musheno argued that street-level workers were significantly motivated by the influence of their own moral judgments in applying the laws and procedures they were entrusted with. They relied heavily on their personal understanding of their clients— "fairness and justice mean responding to citizen-clients based on their perceived worth" (Maynard-Moody and Musheno 2003: 93–94). In *Street-Level Leadership: Discretion and Legitimacy in Front-Line Public Service* (1998), Janet Coble-Vinzant and Lane Crothers also emphasized that public sector workers in daily contact with the population derived a good proportion of their satisfaction with work from the importance of their role. In his *People Processing: The Street-Level Bureaucrat in Public Service Bureaucracies* (1979), Jeffrey M. Prottas focused on how degrees of discretion shaped job satisfaction. Four groups of people motivated to perform public service were identified in a study of seven states in the United States: samaritans, communitarians, patriots and humanitarians. Economic rewards ranked low, as did involvement in policymaking. "We are left with vivid images of people helping people—not principals and agents chasing customers" (Brewer, Selden and Facer 2000: 262). It is worth noting that the vast majority of front-line public servants in these studies occupied positions that required client relationships, not routine, impersonal customer contacts. In Canada, the work of Carroll and Siegel, *Service in the Field* (1999), captured more of the latter functions, and depicted an unsatisfied work force struggling in vain for some discretion and latitude in applying rules and procedures.

Governments have sought recently to improve their understanding of their employees but, significantly, not with the clear purpose of creating a better service culture to the public. The Alberta government was a pioneer in conducting employee surveys in the 1990s, but most provinces would hesitate a long time before undertaking such work (Newfoundland and Labrador, Prince Edward Island and Quebec still do not survey employees systematically. Nuvavut has apparently surveyed its employees, but no data is publicly available.).

The British Columbia Auditor-General first focused on the study of employee engagement in 2000–01 and published its results in 2002. The report tied the results to a service culture and commented that:

...a well performing public service also requires employees who are 'engaged'—that is intellectually and emotionally involved in their work and organization. Engaged employees are proud of their contribution to the success of their organization, team or work units; they speak positively about their organizations to friends, family, acquaintances, customers and other stakeholders; and demonstrate an intense desire to remain a part of their organization (British Columbia 2002–03: 2).

The BC Auditor-General's report even pointed to some innovative solutions. "In British Columbia's public service the culture should, in our view, be citizen-centred," it declared.

That is, employees should highly value citizen interest and act on new ways to make service better for their clients. A successful citizen-centred culture is one that empowers people; that encourages [them] to be innovative and to communicate openly; and that focuses on satisfying, to the extent possible, both clients and the general public, through continuous improvement (Ibid., 24).

The BCA-G, borrowing from the consulting firm Hewitt Associates, equated 'commitment' with 'engagement' as defined as "the state of intellectual and emotional involvement in one's work and organization". Engaged employees were most likely to 'stay' with their employer and not seek employment elsewhere, 'say' positive things about their employers and be proud to serve in their functions (Ibid., 23). To sharpen its focus the drivers of employee engagement, the BCA-G, identified the drivers of employee satisfaction as:

- leaders they respect and trust;
- interesting and meaningful work;
- open and respectful relationships with their clients, co-workers and supervisors;
- opportunities to develop new skills and advance in their career;
- recognition for work well done;
- physical security;
- economic security; and
- balance between work and home life (Ibid., 24).

In 2007 the Government of New Brunswick—since the early 1990s a leader in raising awareness around customer service via its Service New

Brunswick (SNB) agency—surveyed its employees directly on their drivers of satisfaction. It concluded that the five most important factors for its employees (in order of importance) were "being treated with respect and consideration;" "stimulating and interesting work;" "job security;" "working with a supervisor I respect;" and "opportunities for advancement" (New Brunswick 2007: 7). The similarities between the British Columbia and New Brunswick studies were obvious, but in focusing more closely on front-line employees, SNB found that its employees differed somewhat from the general response. In order of importance, "being treated with respect" was most critical, followed by "opportunities for advancement," "job security" and "working conditions". What was most striking was that Service New Brunswick employees were less likely to choose "opportunities to see my ideas adopted and applied" (15 percent compared to 20 percent generally); "opportunities to influence outcomes in the province" (14 percent versus 22 percent generally); "being able to make my own decisions on how to do my job" (22 percent compared to 34 percent generally); "having fun at work" (27 percent compared to 22 percent generally); and "work life balance" (33 percent versus 28 percent generally) (Ibid.).

In 2006, six governments—British Columbia, Alberta, Saskatchewan, Ontario, Nova Scotia and the Government of Canada—agreed to develop a joint approach to measuring and comparing employee engagement on the assumption that 'engagement' was equal to satisfaction *and* commitment put together. The working team took stock of what the various jurisdictions had been surveying and agreed to identify a common working model on employee engagement from which common survey questions would be distilled. The jurisdictions also agreed to share results and to discuss possible strategies that could be implemented to improve results (Anonymous 2006).

The model identified 'engaged' employees as being 'satisfied' with overall employment; satisfied with their organization; wishing to serve or perform at high levels; willing to recommend their organization to others; willing to stay with their organization; and feeling pride with their organization.

Engaged employees would be measured on how they answered the following statements:

- Overall, I am satisfied in my work as a [government] employee;
- I am satisfied with my ministry/development;
- I am inspired to give my very best;
- I would recommend the [employer] as a great place to work;

- I would prefer to stay with the [employer] even if offered a similar job elsewhere; and
- I am proud to tell people I work for the [employer].

The amalgams of various scores on these questions were expected to generate an 'index'. Since then, not all governments have followed the recipe—and few of them have been willing to disclose publicly the results of their surveys.

General results

Are employees 'engaged', and therefore more likely to deliver better customer-satisfaction results? The first results showed the average inter-jurisdictional index average of 61 percent in 2006 and 65.5 percent in 2007 (Nova Scotia 2007: 250). Although some results for 2008 were available at the time of writing, they were not sufficient to constitute a reliable average.

In its first survey of 2002, the BC Auditor-General reported that 50 percent of surveyed employees were satisfied with their work. Unfortunately the BC study did not break down the level of occupation of respondents, making it difficult to isolate the percentage of people who were actually front-line workers, let alone people dealing significantly with the public. It calculated the 'engagement' level at 59 percent of employees—notably less than the Hewitt Associates study of the 'top 50' organizations to work for in Canada, which received an average rating of 79 percent (British Columbia 2002–03: 36).

The BCA-G repeated the survey two years later—at a time when the BC government undertook significant restructuring that entailed layoffs and hiring freezes—and reported the results in its 2004–05 report. This time, the engagement rating was recorded at 53 percent, 6 percent lower than the first report. This was a source of alarm: "In our view, these findings should concern government. With employees who are only moderately engaged, government is not likely receiving the best performance possible from its staff" (British Columbia 2004–05: 43). Remarkably results in most sub-categories of job satisfaction were consistent with those recorded in the first survey.

British Columbia's effort in surveying was taken over by the public service agency (BCPSA) and its survey of government employees in 2005/06 recorded a score of 58. The result in 2006–07 was 63 (British Columbia

2007a: 24). In 2008 the result showed a dramatic improvement, recording a 68.4 percent engagement rate—even though only 61 percent of respondents said they were satisfied with their work, and that the same level would stay in their jobs even if a similar job were offered to them elsewhere, and 50 percent of respondents said they were satisfied with their organizations (British Columbia 2008a: i).

Results were more consistently positive in Alberta. The Government of Alberta instituted its annual Corporate Employee Survey in 1996, but did not focus on 'engagement' until 2006. Its first employee engagement index report recorded a score of 69 in that year, 68 in 2007 and 71 in 2008. (Alberta 2008). Results on the key engagement questions were fairly consistent over the three year span, with generally higher results than other jurisdictions. Eighty percent of respondents said they were satisfied "overall" with their work, while 68 percent said they were satisfied with their department. Sixty-seven percent of respondents said they were "inspired to give their very best" and 72 percent said they were "proud to tell people they worked for the Government of Alberta". Although 60 percent said they felt "valued" as a Government of Alberta employee, 70 percent said they would recommend the Government of Alberta as a "great place" to work (Ibid.).

The Government of Manitoba conducted a first survey among its employees in 1998. Staff 'satisfaction' levels in Manitoba were remarkably positive in light of the dramatic changes to the bureaucracy during the 1990s. In 2001, 62 percent of the Manitoba respondents said they were satisfied with their departments. In 2004, 77 percent of staff indicated that they were satisfied with their jobs and 75 percent reported being satisfied in working for their department. Most of the staff reported being proud of their department and proud to be a part of the Manitoba civil service. They said they would recommend government employment to others. The Manitoba government offered an analysis on the top drivers of staff satisfaction that demonstrated a remarkable level of consistency over the decade. It concluded that recognition and appreciation, clarity of mandate, authority on the job, balance and meaningful work were the most important aspects of the job. No breakdown was offered on how results from front-line workers differed from the general results. While no 'engagement index' was used, the Manitoba questions were sufficiently similar to the agreed questions of 2004 to speculate that it would be in the high-60/low-70 range like in Alberta (Manitoba 2005: 5).

The Government of Nova Scotia began monitoring employee engagement systematically in 2004. The first two reports reported uncertainty in the ranks: "most government employees are neither actively engaged nor actively disengaged in their work" (Nova Scotia 2005:11). Results were more positive in the following years. In 2006, 67.3 percent of respondents were classified as 'engaged', and that score changed by 6.4 percent to 71.6 percent in 2007—results remarkably similar to those of Alberta and Manitoba. The report that year was even able to pinpoint employees who were more likely to be 'committed' or 'less committed' (Nova Scotia 2007: 22). Typically, people in management, women, term employees, employees with fewer than two years experience and employees 29 years or younger or 55 years or older were most committed. Among the less committed were men, members of the Canadian Union of Public Employees, and people employed in corrections. As with Manitoba or Alberta, no breakdown was offered to distinguish the views of front-line workers from the general employee population on this score.

In 2006 the Government of the Northwest Territories (GNWT) launched an employee satisfaction and engagement survey and repeated it again early in 2008. In 2008, employees of the GNWT generally showed a high degree of job satisfaction and engagement, and the report offered some breakdown according to occupation. When asked if they were satisfied with their job, 68.4 percent of administrative workers said yes, 3.4 percent less than the average. Asked if they were satisfied with the organization, 58 percent responded yes, 2.6 percent more than the average. Similar results were obtained when asking if the employee was "satisfied with my employment" (Northwest Territories 2008).

When the GNWT survey asked if employees were "proud to tell people I work for this organization", 71.5 percent of administrative workers responded affirmatively; 68.5 percent of total respondents said the same. When asked if they would "stay with the organization even if offered a similar job elsewhere", 53.1 percent answered yes; 49.1 percent of the total respondents said the same. When asked if "people in this organization are inspired to give their very best", 50.4 percent of the administrative group respondents said yes. Asked if "people in this organization strive to improve results", 63.1 percent of administrators agreed versus 59.5 percent in the total employee population. When asked if they were "satisfied with their workload", 55.2 percent of administrative workers said yes; 60.7 percent said the same in the total employee population. The results for both years were similar, and although no precise 'index' was given, an average of the key six questions yields a result of 61 percent, consistent with Alberta, Manitoba and Nova Scotia (Ibid.).

The Government of Saskatchewan undertook a comprehensive survey in 2003 and again at the end of 2005, delivering its latest results in early 2006. Again, scores for service employees were not isolated. The questions posed were somewhat different than other jurisdictions, but essentially aimed at capturing the same sentiment. In terms of employee satisfaction, 76 per cent of respondents said that they took pride in working for their departments and in working for the Saskatchewan public service (SPS). Fifty percent of respondents were optimistic about their future in the Saskatchewan public service and 61 percent would recommend working in the SPS to family or friends. Sixty-eight percent had no plans to leave, even if they had an opportunity to do so. The results showed a slight decline from the results obtained in the 2003 survey but by and large compared favourably with other public sectors (Hay Group Insight 2006: 41).

Based on only four of the six 'satisfaction' questions, the engagement index result for Saskatchewan in 2006 would have hovered around the high 60s/low 70s, or in the range attained by employees in neighbouring Alberta and Manitoba.

New Brunswick conducted its first employee survey in June 2007 and, unique among governments, isolated results for Service New Brunswick. Government-wide, 80 percent responded that they were generally satisfied with their work, and 81 percent of surveyed employees in Service New Brunswick said they were satisfied. SNB employees were also considerably more satisfied with their department: 71 percent (65 percent for New Brunswick government employees generally) indicated that they were satisfied with their department. (New Brunswick 2007: 12). For the rest of the results on general satisfaction, SNB results were fairly consistent with those recorded from all government employees. Seventy-seven percent of SNB respondents said they were proud to tell people they worked for their employers, slightly more than the 75 percent who said so in the general employee population. Sixty-seven percent of SNB respondents said that they would stay with SNB even if offered a similar job elsewhere (66 percent of the general respondents said the same). Sixty-eight percent of SNB employees would recommend their ministry as an "excellent place to work" versus 64 percent generally. Based on results obtained on the five of the six critical 'satisfaction' questions, SNB employees would have recorded a score of 73 on the engagement index, slightly higher than the Government of New Brunswick score of 70, but also consistent with most provinces (Ibid.).

The Government of Ontario conducted two surveys explicitly concerned with employee engagement. The most recent, done in 2007, recorded an average index score of 65.97. Service employees were not isolated in the results, but it is worth reporting that the Ministry of Government Services, which houses ServiceOntario, registered a 67.28 score. Seventy-five percent of these respondents agreed that they "strive to improve my ministry's results" and 64 percent say that they are "inspired to give my very best." Of the respondents, 65 percent said they were "proud to work for my ministry", although only 44 percent agreed that they were "satisfied with their ministry" (Ipsos-Reid 2007).

The Yukon Territory reported on its first survey of employees in 2007 and recorded a 64 on the engagement index. Seventy-two percent said they were satisfied with their work as a Government of Yukon employee while 68 percent of respondents said they were satisfied with their jobs, and fewer still (54 percent) reported being satisfied with their department. Fifty-seven percent of respondents said they were proud to tell people they were employees of the territorial government and roughly the same number (55 percent) would stay with the government if they were offered similar work elsewhere. A year later, the situation had deteriorated as the engagement score dropped to 60 percent. Sixty-four percent of respondents pronounced themselves satisfied with their work as Yukon employees, 62 percent were satisfied with their jobs and 49 percent were satisfied with their government. While the same number said they were proud to tell people they worked for the Yukon, all the recorded results showed a substantial drop in satisfaction between 2007 and 2008 (Yukon 2008).

The Government of Canada conducted a public service employee survey in 1999, 2002, 2005 and 2008. Averaging the scores for the six questions, the 2008 score of employee engagement was 70.5 (Canada 2008a). It was lower than the result recorded in 2005—when, according to the government, 90 percent of Government of Canada employees were "committed" to their work—but still high in comparison with provincial scores. The 2005 score was similar to that of 2002 when no less than 96 percent of those surveyed said that they were "strongly committed to making their organization successful" and over 80 percent said that their organization was a "good place to work" (Canada 2005a). Working from the data, however, one observer calculated the employee engagement index of the 54 federal departments and agencies and drew a different picture. The highest score was achieved by the Canadian Environmental Assessment Agency with a 68.9 percent score and the lowest score was obtained by the Correctional Service of Canada with 46 percent. Service Canada was ranked 51st on the list with a score of 52.3 percent (Cole 2008).

Unfortunately, the 2008 survey does not allow for a straight comparison. Ottawa only asked four of the six key questions for the engagement survey (leaving out "I am inspired to give my very best" and "I am proud to tell people I work for [employer]" and by modifying the question "I would prefer to stay with the [employer] even if offered a similar job elsewhere" with "I would prefer to remain with my department or agency, even if a comparable job was available elsewhere in the federal Public Service". Allowing for the latter question, the engagement score for those employees most likely dealing with customers on a daily basis would be 55.5 percent, or roughly consistent with the result obtained in 2005 (Canada 2008a).

In its 2008 survey of employees, the federal government's Treasury Board Secretariat reported that 28 percent of respondents strongly agreed with the statement that they were "satisfied with my department or agency" while another 40 percent somewhat agreed (Ibid., question 60). Results for Service Canada were somewhat lower with 23 percent recording a "strongly agree", and 40 percent recording a "somewhat agree". Indeed, to drill down further, the results for the Citizen Service Branch of Service Canada revealed an even lower rate of satisfaction with 17 percent strongly agreeing to being satisfied, and 36 percent in agreement. For the Citizen Service Branch, 53 percent of respondents seem to be satisfied with their department.

To focus more clearly on the function of the employee, it also posed as a statement "I get a sense of satisfaction from my work" (Ibid., question 9). Thirty-five percent of respondents strongly agreed with the statement and another 42 percent agreed. The results for Service Canada (and the Citizen Service Branch) were almost exactly the same. There seemed to be a high degree of consistency.

While it is always difficult to draw grand conclusions from general scores, it is clear from the publicly available sampling that 'engagement' indexes have ranged from a low of 53 percent in British Columbia in 2004 to a high of 71 percent in Alberta in 2007. How much of this is actually explained by workplace issues is an open question, however. If governments are retrenching in terms of support and tools and menace pay freezes, morale will likely suffer. It is also likely that if government is generous in wage increases, training subsidies and benefits, morale will improve and so will public sector motivation and engagement (Vandenabeele 2009; Leisink and Steijn 2009; Ritz 2009). Other factors can also play a role—a secure position in government, for instance, can be more keenly appreciated if the local economy flounders.

Finally, there are issues of interpretation over what actually constitutes 'engagement'. All the surveys calculate that if a respondent 'agrees' with a certain proposition, they are 'engaged'. If, however, only 'strongly agree' responses are considered as truly constituting 'engagement', then results would be dramatically lower. Studies have distinguished between levels of normative (low), continuance (medium), and affective (high) commitment (Belcourt and Taggar 2002), and there is little doubt that the score for engagement could be dissected so that is has greater meaning. Other structural measures, of course, could also be considered. Absenteeism, for instance, is usually considered the leading indicator of engagement. Employees who tend to miss work repeatedly generally are considered to have a lower commitment to their jobs. These rates are not made public.

Nevertheless, it seems clear that the average engagement index in government probably hovers around the mid-60s as a general rule (the score for the five participating provinces—it is worth noting that not all of them have issued separate reports—was 63 in 2007–08 (Yukon 2008). All the same, comparisons are very difficult to make. The BC Auditor-General's attempt to benchmark against Canada's 'top 50' employers was simply misguided. Most of the 'top 50' component companies are self-selected by volunteering survey results and most firms that earn the 'top' moniker are simply not comparable to the size and mission of the public service. It is also worth noting that the Gallup organization conducted a broad survey on work engagement and found that typically only thirty percent of respondents were engaged in their work (Gallup Consulting 2008). The multiplicity of engagement measurement methods makes it indeed difficult to compare indexes.

Working with clients

While general indexes can be useful, a fuller picture of job satisfaction can be obtained by examining various details of the working life of employees. The customer-employee link was first discussed in the context of Canadian public sector scholarship in 1991. In an article in *Canadian Public Administration* Rémi Lacasse showed that "satisfied, inspired, enthusiastic employees are bettered equipped to satisfy customers. In return, satisfying customers is very satisfying to employees. By improving one, the other is almost automatically also improved" (Lacasse 1991: 485; Swiss 1992).

Some governments have been sufficiently concerned about this issue to ask about it directly. The first study by the BCA-G reported that 71 percent enjoyed "working with their clients" (British Columbia 2002–03: 35).

Service New Brunswick recorded that 74 percent of employees agreed that they had the support to offer high quality services to their clients versus 67 percent of the general employee population, and 67 percent said that innovation was valued in the workplace versus 64 percent generally (New Brunswick 2007: 12). In Ontario, 70 percent agreed with the proposition that "people in my work unit place a high value on providing good service to our customers" (Ipsos-Reid 2007) while in Saskatchewan, 67 percent agreed that "delivering on service excellence is usually practiced in your workplace" (Hay Group Insight 2006).

The BC surveys conducted by the provincial Auditor-General (no questions on this topic were posed by BC Stats in 2006 and 2007) asked respondents if they "often do more than what's necessary to help our clients" and 87 percent of respondents said yes. The first BCA-G was told that 75 percent of respondents focused "on their client's needs and do more than they are required to do in order to help clients". But when asked if "this department really inspires me to do my best work", only 45 percent agreed. "We found that…British Columbia's public service employees are only moderately engaged in their work", the Comments section of the report declared:

> That is, they are just as dedicated to serving their clients, but are not as proud of where they work or as committed to staying…We believe these findings should be of serious concern to the government" (British Columbia 2004–05: 8).

The report did not break down the results of the survey, but did note that "managers were consistently more satisfied with their work environment than other occupational groups…this pattern has not changed from our 2001 survey" (Ibid., 9).

In Manitoba staff surveys, responses pertaining to client/citizen service were very positive and showed some significant improvements over the 2001 results. According to the 2005 report, "staff remain highly committed to client service and believe that service excellence is a priority in their work" (Manitoba 2005: 3). Although staff reported high levels of commitment to service, fewer agreed that there was extensive support for improving service delivery from senior management when compared to 2001. The 2004 report showed that most staff saw things improving on the service front since 2001. Approximately 60 percent of staff felt their department had made changes to improve services in comparison to only 36 percent of staff in 2001. Respondents also reported high levels of management support and commitment to service (Manitoba 2005).

In Saskatchewan, fewer agreed with the quality of services being offered. Forty-eight percent agreed with the statement that "I believe citizens and clients are satisfied with the services provided by my department"; 34 percent agreed with the statement that "I believe citizens and clients are satisfied with the services provided by the Saskatchewan public service". All the same, 59 percent agreed that "my department insists on high quality work by its employees" (Hay Group Insight 2006). In the Yukon, 83 percent of respondents agreed that they "strive to improve" their department's results (Yukon 2008), but in both the 2007 and 2008 surveys, 61 percent of Yukon employees agreed with the statement that "I have the support at work to provide a high level of service" (Ibid.).

The 2005 federal survey examined this issue in more detail. Its report showed that 79 percent of employees "indicated that their work unit had clearly defined client service standards", 8 percent more than results generally attained and that 76 percent "believed that their work unit regularly applied these standards", 9 percent more than the general average. The report also found that 60 percent of employees considered that there were mechanisms for relaying client feedback to decision makers, 5 percent more than the average. A remarkable degree of respondents (74 percent) indicated that they had sufficient discretion to "adapt their services to client needs" (Canada 2005a, question 75).

The 2008 survey posed a more general statement: "My work unit provides high quality service to its clients". To that proposition, 49 percent strongly agreed, while 36 percent agreed. The relevance of the question is dubious, because different definitions of 'clients' could be interpreted, ranging from the Prime Minister to young parents seeking a social insurance number for a child. The question of focusing on services to individual citizens as clients or customers was not asked. Regardless, the results recorded for Service Canada were almost exactly the same. Its Citizen Service Branch's results were slightly below, with 44 percent strongly agreeing and 40 percent somewhat agreeing (Canada 2008a, question 31).

The issue of improving the rapport with customers is not easy to resolve. Government service providers must deal with Canadians from all walks of life that have little choice in dealing with government. (Unlike private sector counterparts who deal with self-selected clients who seek some sort of betterment and are willing to pay for it.) The task of serving demanding clients—who may resent bureaucracy and its 'red tape', who are impatient with process, and who may have little understanding of the implications of their complex demands—can be daunting. In this regard, the results of the surveys display a public service that is remarkably at ease with its clientele. Government employers can improve on the results, of course, by managing contact hours; multiplying channels of communication; generally spending more to accelerate service and reduce waiting times; improve accessibility; and reducing work stress so that staff is always courteous and pleasant. This requires substantial investments and a cost justification that so far has not been made public.

Scholars have long suggested that a key to improving the interface between the service provider and the customer is to provide more discretion to the employee in resolving issues (Carroll and Siegel 1999). This issue is not without controversy. On the practical side, the ability to reach a compromise can be empowering to the employee and contribute to professional fulfillment. But clearly there are rigorous limits to the amount of latitude possible. The public service must be seen as delivering similar services to all with no preferential treatment. Some observers have taken serious issue with the amount of latitude already provided, raising issues around threats to 'democracy' that can be engendered by the practice, as well as a distortion of what was directed from the executive ranks (Sossin 2002).

Working relationships with co-workers

Most workers will evaluate their position based on their lived experience with colleagues and direct supervisors. On this count, results show in many cases a remarkable level of satisfaction. In its first study, the BC Auditor-General reported that 78 percent were satisfied with their co-workers (British Columbia 2002–03: 35). Six years later, the score of 81 was recorded (British Columbia 2007a: 12). In New Brunswick 96 percent of SNB respondents in 2006 agreed that they had "positive working relationships with co-workers", slightly more than the 93 percent recorded in the general employee population.

In the 2008 survey of its employees, the Government of the Northwest Territories reported that 88 percent of respondents felt that they had "positive working relationships with their co-workers". Over 86 percent felt their work contributed to the "achievement of department goals" and also felt that their job was suitable to their skills (Northwest Territories 2008: 35). The GNWT study did not isolate personnel who worked in services to the

public, but did identify 'administration' as a distinct occupation group—
the catch-all category that would most likely capture service employees.
The results for this category were remarkably consistent with the average;
85 percent agreed that they had positive working relationships with their
co-workers and had a "positive relationship with the person they reported
to". The Yukon registered similar figures. Eighty-six percent reported that
they enjoyed positive relationships with their co-workers in 2007 (84 percent said the same in 2008) but only 59 percent agreed that there was good
communication between members of the unit (Yukon 2008).

In the 2006 Saskatchewan survey of employees, 62 percent of respondents agreed that "promoting good co-operation is usually practiced in your
workplace". When asked about their working environment, 89 percent
reported having "positive working relationships with co-workers" although,
oddly, only 42 percent reported enjoying "a cooperative atmosphere in your
department" (Hay Group Insight 2006).

Government workers in Manitoba also reported having nourishing relationships with their colleagues. In 2004 over 80 percent indicated that their
co-workers treated them with respect and most staff had been recognized
by their co-workers for a job well done. The report of the survey indicated
that "there was no change in the proportion of staff who felt appreciated
as an employee or who felt that staff was viewed as important resources for
their department when compared to the 2001 results" (Manitoba 2005).
One could go further in friendly Manitoba, where survey results showed
that "approximately 66 percent of survey respondents felt their co-workers were concerned with their well-being" and that trust among colleagues
grew by 17 percent between 2001 and 2004; 45 percent reported distrust
in 2003, compared to 53 percent in 2001 (Ibid.).

The Government of Nova Scotia's 2007 survey did not isolate results
for service workers, but it recorded 87 percent support for the statement
that "the people I work with make an effort to help each other out" and 90
percent for the statement "I have positive working relationships with my
coworkers". But there are kinks in the story. The report itself acknowledged
that members of the Canadian Union of Public Employees were much
less 'engaged' than others. Service Nova Scotia and Municipal Relations
recorded the lowest response rate (23.8 percent) of any ministry, a more
than 50 percent drop since the first survey in 2004, which had earned a
48.6 percent response rate (Nova Scotia 2005: B2).

The Government of Canada broke out the results for Service Canada in
2005 and showed that 80 percent of respondents mostly agreed or strongly

agreed with the proposition that "in my work unit, we work cooperatively as a team" (Canada 2005a: question 34). The results, moreover, were fairly consistent with those achieved in 1999 and 2002. The results in 2008 (question 26) indicated strong agreement, with 78 percent of respondents agreeing with the statement. The Citizen Service Branch of Service Canada scored higher than average with 38 percent of respondents strongly agreeing and 44 percent somewhat agreeing.

Clearly, government workers enjoy each other's company, presenting a workplace culture that is remarkably supportive on a human scale. In this regard, it is doubtful that the public sector workplace poses some sort of threat to customer service or that this key driver of employee satisfaction would require major investment.

Working with supervisors

A critical aspect of employee satisfaction is the relationship with supervisors (Belcourt and Taggar 2002). Inevitably, situations in which the leader-follower rapport is negative lead to poorer performance. The rapport with supervisors is complex. It involves work assignments; support in problem-solving; quality of vision; personal interactions; communication of personal and corporate goals; perceptions of fairness; evaluations; degrees of discretion; and recognition. In Canada, Carroll and Siegel took a different approach and based their *Service in the Field* on a survey that revealed a great deal of distrust of employers.

The BC Auditor-General's 2001 study was concerned about this issue but did not test it directly. Instead, it asked a number of questions that form a composite indication of how employees perceived their supervisors. The survey asked if employees felt recognized by their employers for their work. The results were startling to the BCA-G when it was revealed that only 29 percent of the employees were satisfied with the recognition they received generally and even fewer (27 percent of respondents) believed they received recognition for high-quality client service (British Columbia 2002–03: 44).

In terms of "making good use of my knowledge and abilities", British Columbia earned a 69 percent (compared with 80 percent for the 'top 50' employers). On the critical issue of "I have the authority to make the decisions necessary to do my job well", British Columbia received 62 percent, compared to 79 percent. On the issue of "I have the tools [technology and equipment] I need to do my job well", British Columbia earned 67 percent, compared to 80 percent for the top companies (British Columbia 2002-03: 36). The BC survey of 2007 confirmed some improvement. For instance, 49 percent of respondents agreed that they had been recognized for work well done (British Columbia 2008a: 12). Forty-six percent of respondents said that recognition was "based on merit". Sixty-one percent of respondents agreed that "the person I report to consults me on decisions that affect me" and 60 percent agreed with the statement "the person I report to keeps me informed of things I need to know". Sixty percent of respondents agreed that "a healthy atmosphere [e.g., trust, mutual respect] exists in my work unit". Fifty-five percent of respondents agreed that they were "encouraged to be innovative" in their work (Ibid., 11–12).

The Government of New Brunswick (GNB) focused on many aspects of the leader-follower relationship more directly and in 2007 released some telling general results as well as those of its service agency, Service New Brunswick. Seventy-seven percent of SNB workers indicated that they were satisfied with their supervisors versus 73 percent for the whole of the GNB. Fifty-eight percent of SNB workers said that they received recognition for their work versus 60 percent for the GNB and 66 percent reported that their manager provided regular feedback on their performance versus 62 percent for the general survey. Seventy-five percent said they were "inspired to give my very best" and 68 percent agreed that they had the "opportunity to provide input into decisions that affect my work". Ninety-two percent (90 percent in the GNB) agreed that they understood how their work contributed to the objectives of their department. Slightly fewer SNB workers (64 percent versus 68 percent) believed that they had opportunities to participate in decision making on matters related to their work, but slightly more (78 percent) declared themselves inspired to give their best in their work (75 percent generally) (New Brunswick 2007).

In Service New Brunswick, 82 percent of employees agreed with the statement that "the work expectations placed on me by my manager are reasonable", compared to 78 percent in the general government population (Ibid., 12). Significantly, it was the most important gap in the results. When asked if they trusted the executive in their department, 71 percent of respondents at SNB agreed versus 61 percent in the GNB population. It was roughly the same gap recorded in general satisfaction (71 percent versus 65 percent).

The Manitoba survey of 2004 also tested the relationship between employees and their supervisors. Overall, employees perceived their supervisors in a most favourable light—almost 80 percent indicated their immediate supervisor treated them "fairly and with respect". The majority of respondents even reported that they felt their supervisors were concerned "with their well-being". Manitoba employees showed an appreciation for the fact that there were more opportunities for input into decision making, and 65 percent of respondents agreed that their immediate supervisor showed an interest in their ideas. However, when asked if employee suggestions and ideas are considered, despite their position, fewer staff agreed (55 percent) (Manitoba 2005).

The Manitoba surveys queried whether employees considered that there was an alignment of view between supervisors and staff on priorities. The 2001 survey showed that 39 percent of employees agreed that there was a harmony of views in that their "immediate supervisor communicated clearly with them and understood their supervisor's work expectations". By 2004, that number had climbed to 55 percent of respondents. Also, 44 percent of staff considered that their department had "a clear vision and strategy" in 2001. Three years later, progress was recorded as about half of the respondents felt this way. Indeed, supervisors in Manitoba seemed to perform relatively well compared to department executives. In 2001 it was reported that just over 40 percent of staff surveyed felt confident in the leadership skills of senior management. The 2004 Manitoba survey also showed that employees felt they had a good level of autonomy and authority to conduct their work. Over 70 percent of respondents felt they had a reasonable balance between work and home with the majority of staff agreeing that their work environment supported a work-life balance. Indeed, even the stress level in Manitoba offices seemed well managed. In 2001, 53 percent of respondents agreed that they found their work stressful. That number dropped to 37 percent in 2004, even though employees reported heavier workloads (Ibid.).

The Manitobans were not without frustrations, especially when it came to autonomy. Results in 2004 showed that employees reported more 'red tape' and onerous bureaucratic processes for approvals and decision making that took them away from their primary responsibilities than in 2001. This frustration undoubtedly coloured their response when asked about evaluating the innovativeness of their department. To use the words of the report:

> ...although most survey participants indicated their immediate supervisor encourages creativity and innovation, fewer than 40% agreed their

Department is innovative and willing to take risks. Most staff who participated in the survey felt that 'doing it by the book' was a high priority in the Department. There was however, a slight increase in the proportion of staff who agreed their Department is flexible and can respond to changing needs and circumstances – 51%, up from 46% in 2001 (Manitoba 2005: 10).

In the 2006 Saskatchewan survey, 37 percent agreed that there were "opportunities to communicate to higher levels in the department" and 55 percent agreed that their immediate manager "is sharing information about organizational changes and how they impact your work group". Only 31 percent, however, agreed that their job "provides a chance to have your ideas adopted and put into use". While 41 percent agreed that "when things go well in your job, your contributions are usually recognized", 54 percent reported that their "immediate manager is recognizing you when you do a good job". Forty-one percent said they agreed with the statement that "your immediate manager is giving you feedback on the kind of job you are doing on a regular basis" and 53 percent agreed that "I receive enough feedback on how well I do my work". In the 2006 Saskatchewan survey of employees, 61 percent of respondents were "inspired to give my very best" (Hay Group Insight 2006).

In terms of autonomy, 38 percent of the Saskatchewan employees said in 2006 that they "had the resources they need to do a good job in their department". Sixty percent reported that they "had all the information I need to do my job well", 76 percent took pride in working for the Saskatchewan public service and 68 percent had no plans to leave.

On the issue of supervision, 61 percent of respondents in Saskatchewan agreed with the statement that their "immediate manager is helping resolve job-related problems" and 63 percent agreed that their "immediate manager is listening to what you have to say". Fewer people were as favourable on other aspects of the supervision. Between 55 percent and 57 percent of respondents agreed with the propositions that their immediate manager was "setting clear work priorities and objectives"; was a "role model of behaviours expected of staff"; was "dealing fairly with everyone—playing no favourites"; and "taking action on your problems or complaints" (Ibid.).

In its 2006 Corporate Employee Survey, the Government of Alberta asked "To what extent do you agree or disagree that you are satisfied with how clearly work expectations are communicated to you?" The recorded result was that 65 percent of employees agreed they were satisfied with how clearly work expectations are communicated to them, a decrease of one percentage point from the 2005 result of 66 per cent. In 2007 that result was 68 percent. Sixty-four percent of respondents agreed that they had the "support to provide a high level of service", 71 percent were "satisfied with the quality of supervision" and 92 percent agreed that they had "positive relationships with co-workers". Eighty-three percent responded that they had "a sense of personal accomplishment in your work" (Alberta 2008). The 2007 Alberta survey queried new areas, and here the senior leadership fared less well. Fifty-eight percent of respondents considered that senior leadership demonstrated interest in well being, and only 53 percent considered that it provided clear direction. Less than half (46 percent) considered that senior management made timely decisions (Ibid.).

In Nova Scotia, 80 percent of respondents agreed with the notion that "my supervisor considers my work-related ideas" and agreed in the same number for the claim that "I have access to training opportunities" (Nova Scotia 2007: 16). Eighty-one percent of respondents agreed that they could "talk openly with my supervisor about my work" and that they had a "positive working relationship with the person I report to", and 80 percent reported that they were "proud to work as a civil servant" (Ibid., 17).

In the GNWT survey of 2008, 69.3 percent of administrators agreed that the "person I report to is an effective leader"—5.6 percent above average. The survey asked workers if they felt they received meaningful recognition for work well done and 55.6 percent responded affirmatively, 2.2 percent more than the average. Asked if they agreed with the statement that they had "the support to provide a high level of service", 64.7 percent answered yes, 3.2 percent more than the average. Fifty-eight percent of administration employees had confidence in their senior leadership, which was 2.7 percent above average. Some 61.7 percent of this group also felt that they had "opportunities to provide meaningful input into decisions" that affected their work (Northwest Territories 2008). The Yukon survey of 2007 also registered similar figures: 64 percent pronounced themselves satisfied with the quality of supervision they received. Remarkably, that score was improved by a dramatic 10 percent increase in 2008, with 74 percent expressing satisfaction. Senior leadership fared less well. While 54 percent of respondents identified themselves as having confidence in the senior leadership of their department in 2007, only 47 percent felt the same way a year later. Indeed only 37 percent agreed with the statement that the senior leadership made "timely decisions". In 2008, less than half of the respondents (46 percent) believed that senior leadership was "genuinely interested in the well being of employees" and only 40 percent agreed that the department provided clear direction (Yukon 2008: 24).

Results for Ontario in the 2007 survey were more positive, with 54 percent reporting that there is "good communication among the members of my work unit" and 37 percent saying that "in my work unit", the right information gets to the right people at the right time". Worse, 26 percent reported that "essential information flows effectively from senior leadership to staff". The reverse was also true, however: 29 percent reported that "essential information flows effectively from staff to senior leadership". All the same, 50 percent of respondents to the Ontario survey reported that "I have support at work to provide a high level of service". Sixty-two percent said that "I have the independence I need to make decisions about my daily work"; 43 percent said that "innovation is valued in my work unit" and "I am encouraged to take reasonable, defensible risks in doing my job" (Ipsos-Reid 2007).

In terms of the Government of Canada, employees in 2005 seemed to report a good relationship. Among Service Canada employees, 62 percent agreed that they received "useful feedback from my immediate supervisor on my job performance", slightly less than the average result. Scores were above average on the proposition that "I can count on my immediate supervisor to keep his or her promises" with 75 percent of respondents agreeing (Canada 2005a: questions 19, 20). Although the results attained by Service Canada were generally less positive than the average, they were not significantly lower. By and large, employees felt they received adequate recognition for the work they did (66 percent), and 72 percent of employees overwhelmingly felt that their supervisors kept them informed of "the issues affecting their work" (Ibid., questions 21, 22). It was not surprising to see that 89 percent of Service Canada employees were "proud of the work carried out in my work unit" (Ibid., questions 19, 20). The results in 2008 were similar: 39 percent of respondents in the Citizen Service Branch strongly agreed with the statement that "I can count on my immediate supervisor to keep his or her promises"—another 28 percent somewhat agreed (Canada 2008a: question 34). Fifty-two percent (much higher than the average for Service Canada and the Public Service of Canada) reported that they strongly agreed that they could "disagree with my immediate supervisor on work-related issues without fear of reprisal"—another 25 percent somewhat agree (Ibid., question 37).

The relationship with supervisors is a critical driver of job satisfaction (Belcourt and Taggar 2002), and in this regard the employee culture seems fairly positive in those areas that surveyed their employees directly on the question. Can results be expected to climb much higher? It would be difficult. Unlike the private sector where supervisors can play a critical role in determining salary, public sector managers must comply with a host of rules, statutes and labour agreements. It is worth noting that remuneration is rarely addressed in these surveys—perhaps with good reason; (the exception is the 2007 British Columbia survey which did ask for feedback on salary, and 38 percent of respondents agreed that they were fairly paid for their work). Supervisors in the public sector, however, have few things to offer particularly effective employees. Financial bonus structures for work well done are rare; discretion in accomplishing work is limited; and recognition will only go so far. Moreover, public servants working closely with the public are comparatively well paid compared with private sector workers doing equivalent work, and certainly much better paid than workers in the third sector. How can supervisors do a better job of recognizing and rewarding engagement when they have practically nothing to offer? It is clear that governments wishing to improve on this aspect of the public value chain would have to invest heavily with little reasonable expectation that the financial improvement would generate substantial gains.

Career opportunities

It is commonly agreed that the prospect of career opportunities is an important factor for employees in determining their satisfaction with their job. If the position is perceived to be a 'dead end', some employees may be less accepting of some of the difficulties inherent to the position. The results on this question could be perceived as a setback, but it poses particular challenges for interpretation. Many individuals who are content and fulfilled by their position may not be looking for job opportunities, or even be sensitive to their existence. Many employees are hesitant to leave the ranks of public service unions. Finally, many members of the front-line public service may be conscious of the fact that their skills may not be applicable elsewhere in the bureaucracy. Nevertheless, the issue is important to monitor in terms of trends, but it is not widely surveyed.

For instance, the BCA-G's first study showed that only 28 percent agreed that there were "enough opportunities…to advance in their career" (British Columbia 2002–03: 7). The second BC report noted an improvement in the situation, but still only 36 percent found it adequate and only 38 percent considered that the way promotions were being managed was fair (Ibid., 48). There was noticeable improvement on this front. In the 2007 survey, 63 percent of respondents agreed with the statement "my organization supports my work related learning and development" but fewer (52 percent) agreed with the statement that "I have adequate opportunities to develop my skills" (Ibid., 12).

In the GNWT survey of 2006, 41.5 percent of administrative workers agreed that they had "opportunities for career growth within the organization", much less than the 50.1 percent score recorded for the whole of the GNWT (Northwest Territories 2008). New Brunswick's 2007 survey scored a similar result with 44 percent of SNB employees (41 percent of employees in the Government of New Brunswick) considering that they had opportunities for advancement in their own department. Forty-two percent of New Brunswick employees agreed that they had opportunities for advancement in the government generally versus 40 percent (New Brunswick 2007: 12).

Some jurisdictions asked questions regarding career 'development' as opposed to 'opportunities'. In both the 2007 and 2008 surveys, 50 percent of Yukon respondents agreed with the statement "I have opportunities for career growth with the Government of Yukon" (Yukon 2008: 24).

In Manitoba, the majority of staff surveyed in 2004 indicated that their immediate supervisor supported their career development and most felt their job gave them the opportunity to do their best work. However, only 56 percent of survey participants indicated they had the opportunity to develop and apply skills to enhance their career. When survey participants were asked what they felt was a top priority for improvement, training and development was frequently cited in the comments provided. Although Manitoba staff would still like to see improvements to training, as well as development and advancement opportunities, almost 80 percent agreed that their skills, knowledge and commitment are used in their work (a dramatic improvement when compared to the 59 percent recorded in 2001). When compared to results attained in 2001, there was a significant increase in staff who felt their job was important, while over 80 percent of survey respondents agreed their job is challenging (Manitoba 2005).

In the 2005 Saskatchewan survey, 45 percent said that their department was "providing the training you need to help you handle your present job more effectively". Only 33 percent agreed that "your present job provides a chance to learn new skills and develop your talents" (Hay Group Insight 2006).

In the 2006 Alberta survey, 77 percent of employees responded that their ministry provided "work related learning and development"—a substantial five percent increase since the question was first asked in 2005 (Alberta 2008).

Service Canada employees were less satisfied than the average with 40 percent responding to the proposition that "My department (agency) does a good job of supporting employee career development" (Canada 2005a: question 45). It is worth noting that 51 percent of the general respondents in government agreed with that statement. The Government of Canada survey probed many points in this category, but perhaps the most telling result was in response to the proposition that "Overall, I am satisfied with my career progress in the Public Service". Seventy-four percent of Service Canada respondents were either moderately satisfied or significantly satisfied compared to the 75 percent of government-wide respondents (Ibid., 52). In 2008, the results of the Citizen Service Branch of Service Canada recorded that 20 percent strongly agree and 44 percent somewhat agree with the statement "I have opportunities to develop and apply the skills I need to enhance my career." That score was consistent with the department average and the general public service average (Ibid., question 20).

Training opportunities

It is fair to conclude that employees across Canada feel as though they need more training and development opportunities. Kenneth Kernaghan noted early that training was essential to empowerment and to the transformation of culture (Kernaghan 1992). Most of the training in government is done by peers through informal mentoring and orientation to the job. Many departments have adopted a wider range of training opportunities including online learning, conferences, lectures and learning circles. Integrated Service Delivery (ISD) organizations were created as amalgams of parts of various ministries, thereby creating a challenge in combining various work cultures. To develop 'shared values' governments have been experimenting with new training methods. Service Canada has embraced a full spectrum of learning opportunities for its front-line employees (Flumian, Coe and Kernaghan 2007).

Employees surveyed on this question have consistently indicated that they wished for more training. The first BC survey found that only 41 percent of respondents had received client-service training (British Columbia 2002-03: 44). In the second BC survey of 2004, employees were slightly more satisfied with their development opportunities than in the past. It noted that high performing organizations tend to spend between 3 percent and 5 percent of their payroll expense on training and development. British Columbia was spending no more than 1 percent (British Columbia 2004–05: 47). The situation improved considerably in that the 2007 survey revealed that 56 percent agreed that "the quality of training and development I have received is satisfactory" (British Columbia 2008a: 12).

In a similar time frame, Manitoba employees were also less keen to report satisfaction on this issue, with 56 percent of staff responding in 2001 that they had had opportunities to develop and apply skills to enhance their careers. That result was not much improved upon in the following survey of 2004. The 2005 report noted that "comments provided by staff also suggest that improving and increasing development, advancement and training opportunities should remain a priority" (Manitoba 2005: 13).

A few years later, the Government of New Brunswick 2007 survey reported much more positive results, noting that 71 percent of Service New Brunswick (68 percent in the GNB) agreed that their department supported their "work-related learning and development" (New Brunswick 2007). In the GNWT respondents were asked in 2008 if the organization they worked in supported their "work-related learning and development" and 64.4 percent of administrative workers responded affirmatively, 2.5 percent less than the average (Northwest Territories 2008). In the 2007 survey of Ontario employees, 47 percent agreed that "my ministry supports my work-related learning and development" and 43 percent agreed that "the quality of training and development I have received is very good" but only 38 percent agreed that "the amount of training and development I have received has met my needs" (Ipsos-Reid 2007).

Governments have clearly made attempts to improve their training offerings for their front-line employees. Most programs are focused on intake, ensuring that new employees are familiarized with the technology and the range of services they were hired to offer. The process of 'on-boarding' as a form of basic orientation and training has attracted considerably more attention among service entities. Service BC embarked in 2007 on a mission to develop a standardized and comprehensive training program for new and existing staff based on skill and competency needs as well as rigorous assessments. A number of refresher courses have been offered, depending on the jurisdiction. As new technology is purchased, in-house training is offered in order to optimize the adoption of the new tools. As such, the training is offered by fellow government employees. The delivery of the training program would be a mix of independent learning, online work and limited typical classroom-style approaches with a strong accent on the new hires. The strategy is dependent on continual feedback from staff to determine needs and to assess the training methods. 'Sustainability' and 'accountability' became key elements of the Service BC strategy which ultimately aims at developing effective assessment and training tools (British Columbia 2006a).

As in 1999 and 2002, the 2005 report of the federal public service employee survey showed that 74 percent of employees had "received the training needed to do their jobs." Service Canada employees reported a slightly lower level of satisfaction at 70 percent but, what was more important was that the results had been declining since 1999, when 78 percent had agree with that proposition (Canada 2005a: question 41). The report also found that 59 percent of Service Canada respondents indicated that on-the-job coaching was readily available, compared to 60 percent for the total Government of Canada results. Fifty-four percent of respondents said they had the "opportunities to develop and apply the skills I need to enhance my career" at Service Canada, a score consistent with those recorded in 1999 and 2002.

The Treasury Board Secretariat issued its policy on learning, training and development on January 1, 2006 and its tenets were taken to heart. Indeed, no jurisdiction has gone as far as Canada has in creating a Service Canada College (SCC) in 2006 to take the lead in offering a "Service Excellence Certification Program" for its students. The mission of the college is to "change attitudes, behaviours and mindsets and give our people the tools and, just as importantly, the confidence to engage Canadians in new ways" (Canada 2008b: 1).

The SCC was patterned after the corporate university model that was very popular in large American corporations. It is headed by a 'chief learning officer' who reports directly to the deputy minister of Service Canada and draws its financing from a centrally managed learning investment fund. The curriculum was created from various existing modules and newly created ones, and standardized. Courses can be taken through five learning centres located across Canada, as well as online. The college is anchored in Regina, Saskatchewan. A Service Excellence Certification Program was created to offer a credential. The objective is to cement a 'new culture' of service among front-line employees who were also reclassified at Service Canada from a clerical to a professional designation.

The certification program is awarded after employees have mastered various levels of service excellence. The Mastery Level 1 program introduces

Service Canada employees to the structural elements of the provision of service in terms of basic knowledge, skills and behaviours. The Mastery Level 2 certification program takes place over eighteen months and focuses more on leadership, interpersonal and communication skills. According to Service Canada, "it includes a citizens' forum, experiential learning, site visits, on-the-job coaching, e-learning, a practicum, and a Personal Learning Action Plan" (Ibid., 4).

Employees pursue a 10-day classroom experience at the Regina Service Canada Centre that was built for the purpose of knowledge transfer. In the first two years of the program, over 3,000 learners have completed the Regina experience. It is anticipated that all 20,000 Service Canada employees will eventually undergo the training. Management training has not been an important focus. Courses and qualifications have been the subject of on-going discussions among members of the Institute for Citizen-Centred Service, but little attention has been devoted to job rotation and mentoring. Nevertheless, Service Canada and, indeed, its Citizen Service Branch reported far lower scores than the Public Service of Canada average on the statement "I get the training I need to do my job" (Canada 2005a: question 17). Twenty-one percent of respondents strongly agreed with the statement and 34 percent somewhat agreed in comparison with a score of 25 and 42 for the general average.

In keeping with new public management trends, a great deal of interest has been devoted to training (Borins 2000), but with the exception of the Government of Canada (and to a certain degree, the Government of British Columbia), governments have been content to focus on in-house training of employees focusing on improving performance in their professional roles. The bulk of the training is done through in-house training sessions, participation in process, some external courses and some assignments and projects. In other words, training in this field is directly tied to the experience of the public servant in the role of serving the customer. There is a growing awareness of the need to improve the horizontal and vertical integration of programs (Watad and Ospina 1999), but at the same time there is recognition that there has been relatively little innovation in the service field to drive new learning. The danger is that training programs plateau (Hickey 1996).

Employers are caught in a real dilemma. The cost of training is high and it is clear that governments are having difficulty in justifying the cost of upgrading skills that would not match what governments actually offer in terms of service. The net result has been somewhat of a muddle.

Governments have not been able to adopt key private sector strategies such as job rotations or reassignments, putatively because of labour agreements. Efforts around mentoring and coaching have not been reported. While it is clear that some governments have slowly been creating training focused on customer service, team effectiveness, and continuous improvement (Halvorson and Rodrigues 1996), most of the training they offer is being done independently and online, hardly conducive to creating a service culture.

Conclusion

Can governments create a genuine service culture? The answer is yes, but on condition that there are no expectations that its service culture will ever resemble that of the private sector. The nature of the public service culture—a product of conditions of work, legal obligations, labour unions and work ethics—is vastly different.

The results of various employee satisfaction surveys have demonstrated a number of realities. Most workers are quite satisfied with their jobs. They enjoy their work, enjoy their colleagues, and appear satisfied with their immediate supervisors. Naturally, finer grain surveys will demonstrate where problems exist—typically where supervisors are simply not sufficiently competent and need to be reassigned or dismissed. But given the consistency of results across Canada, these would be exceptions, not rules.

Employees do have gripes that would diminish their satisfaction. Fewer of them are happy with their training, or with the level of discretion they enjoy. Fewer of them also consider that they have all the tools necessary to perform their work. Some have recorded that they are unhappy with their salaries. It is clear that employees in the Citizen Service Branch of Service Canada are marginally less happy with their situations than the average in the Government of Canada. Employees are more likely to be committed to employers who demonstrate a commitment to them, and who demonstrate this with support (Whitener 2001). There is no doubt that all these areas could be improved, but the difficult consideration is in financing the undertaking.

Indeed, it is ironic that the work done so far on the 'public value chain' has not monetized the equation. It is often argued, with reason, that the public sector delivers more than financial rewards. But at some point, departments have to consider the cost of delivering services, not just to ensure that its citizens, clients and customers are satisfied, but also that the taxpayer is well served with cost-efficient and cost-effective services. In this vein, the cost of substantively improving the 'service culture' could be beyond the capacity of most providers. Employee surveys do not indicate a dramatic improvement in satisfaction, although they do indicate, in some cases, a certain consistency. It would seem that the public value chain is so complex in public sector administration as to make the link anything but indirect and thus vulnerable to rival hypotheses of equal grounding.

In light of the generally positive results achieved through the surveys, it was telling that the most popular reading among the people interviewed in the documenting of this chapter (over 2008) was John Fleming and Jim Asplund's *Human Sigma: Managing the Employee-Customer Encounter* (2007). Its message combined a number of strands. The first was the idea that Six Sigma, the management system adopted by a number of companies in the 1980s and 1990s to ensure the consistency of high-quality product, could be refocused on the very human employee-customer encounter. The second strand was an urgent new understanding of that employee-customer encounter as a 'value creation'. The core of their message was that sustained customer satisfaction cannot be attained without managing the issue of employee satisfaction. In terms of strategy, the issues of customer satisfaction and employee satisfaction had to be managed in tandem. The book also argued that local conditions had to prevail over headquarters directives (as much as possible). In other words, employees had to be given as much discretion as possible in helping their customers.

The book could not be popular for its new findings. It offered no examples from Canada, or from the public sector for that matter. None of the examples in the book profiled a unionized workforce. What it did offer was a sort of confirmation that the champions of service improvement were on a special mission. Perhaps the most important sections of the book were those that screamed that measurement was critical to any approach in improving service. That the book was popular as the results of Citizen First 5 were issued—showing that customer satisfaction with government services had plateaued again—was also telling. As governments began to track the opinions of their clientele publicly through the Citizens First exercise, noticeable improvements were recorded. Notwithstanding their doubtful validity, the average score for the 26 services that had been tracked over a 10-year period had increased by 12.5 percent (or 8 points, from 64 to 72). According to Citizens First 5, 37 of the services had trended up and 2 services had recorded lower scores. Thirty-one services showed no statistically significant change, although the study underscored the fact that 15 of those had only been evaluated in 2005 and 2008, so perhaps it was too soon to spot a trend (Erin Research 2008).

How could customer satisfaction levels be static when employee satisfaction seemed to hit new highs? There are many explanations. First, the data presented in this chapter (drawn from public sources) could be too coarse-grained. Although some organizations did make public some data on their service branches or their administrative levels, most did not wish to make this data available to researchers. It could be that data shows that in some organizations with much public interface, employee satisfaction levels are in fact lower, perhaps much lower. It could also be that not enough analysis is devoted to distinguishing results that reveal 'satisfaction' and 'commitment', which are too often conflated (Belcourt and Taggar 2002; Kabachnik 2006). That being said, the results of the service organizations and administration employees were fairly consistent with general results, so there is a limit as to how much the finer data would actually reveal. With time, the conclusions of this study will either be confirmed or refuted. It could also be that the method of surveying employees is not sufficiently likely to capture the real level of engagement. The response rate may not be high enough to provide a full picture of the level of engagement and the quality of the answers can be debatable. A fuller sense of the 'service culture' would be captured with a public account of performance measures, absentee rates and turnover.

In a comparison of the values and commitment of 'knowledge workers' Canadian private sector, public sector and para-public sector employees, researchers found that while public servants did value intellectual stimulation and challenging work more than private sector employees, they were less committed to their organizations than their private sector counterparts (Lyons, Duxbury and Higgins 2006). The study also found that there is no fundamental value predisposition that guides people into a career in one sector or another. Public sector employees are no more altruistic and less self-interested than employees in the private sector. Indeed, the study showed that there was no significant difference in the importance of job security between public and private sector employees.

Clearly, much could be done to resolve some of the issues raised. Better training, for one thing, is being addressed creatively (and expensively) through the Service Canada College, and its structured approach to curriculum will surely be followed closely and either adapted or adopted. Better classification could also be an effective way of recognizing customer service staff. The Government of Canada has taken this step, but the cost of this transition is not clear and may be a real obstacle for most other jurisdictions. Finally, the issue of discretion, which has been identified as critical in the literature, has to be addressed. This does not seem to be a critical factor according to the surveys presented in this chapter, but it stands to reason that executives must accord some degree of latitude to their employees for the latter to feel useful and engaged in their jobs. Because of public service strictures, this will continue to be a Gordian knot.

Human Sigma gave the answer in the idea of creating a new culture of high quality service and it raised ambitions in parts of the public sector. Governments had instinctively started addressing the concerns of employees on workplace issues, and the results made public in various jurisdictions showed that most employees were satisfied with their work. Moreover, the results showed a trend towards consistently better results. The practice of tying survey results to performance pay for deputy ministers, pioneered in British Columbia in 2006, promises even more sensitivity to workplace issues. Clearly, executives across Canada have come to understand that improvements in the workplace on issues such as recognition, supervision and innovation would lead to better results in customer satisfaction.

It could be that governments have already gone as far as possible with the tools at their disposal. The search for new tools (compensation, training, recognition, classification, payment, working conditions) will only cost the treasury more dearly, at a time when many other financial pressures will slow the governments' march. The transition to a more customer-friendly public service has begun and has taken important steps. It could well be that the important phases of the transformation have yet to be imagined.

Based on observation of six agencies in the Australian public service, it has been argued that effective change required: leadership, both administrative and political; an 'appropriate' model of change; room for negotiation and compromise; sufficient resources; and well-planned communication (Stewart and Kringas 2003). In this regard, service departments would have to trust their employees to candidly engage in focus groups with their clients for 'quality dialogue' not just about current services but also about un-serviced needs (Adolfsson and Wikstrom 2007). This is not to deny that service improvement is not possible or desirable. Public service executives, management and employees have a duty to ensure that the citizen's encounter with government is an occasion of courtesy, timely results and fairness of treatment. The pursuit of creating a service culture similar to the private sector, however, will prove to be elusive. It is not evident that culture will lead to more motivation, or that engagement will necessarily lead to better service.

In the end, the only way to genuinely change the service culture will be to rethink policies and procedures, and to develop genuinely 'value-added' products that are likely to attract a clientele instead of citizens wishing to live within the boundaries of the law, and instead of focusing on accessibility issues. On this front, governments have done little. While the work of ensuring courteous, efficient and knowledgeable service cannot end, the objective of a developing a genuine 'service culture' will be elusive.

CHAPTER FOUR

Can We Meet
the Governance Challenge?

Our reviews of service transformation initiatives across Canada suggest that the accommodation of contemporary, integrative, network-based and increasingly electronic public service transformations with traditional, hierarchical governance models is becoming a particularly pressing challenge. The dilemma is as simple as the solution is complex. How do we adapt 19th century hierarchical models of parliamentary governance to the kind of 21st century polycentric, collaborative and open boundary approaches to service delivery that are emerging in many developed polities (Paquet 2004; Kamarck 2004; Allen et al. 2005; Skelcher 2005; Kettl 2005; O'Flynn and Wanna 2008)?

Governance is a broad topic encompassing the structures and processes through which state power is exercised. In recent years there has been increasing attention paid to the participation of non-state actors including citizens, non-profit organizations and firms in state decision making and service delivery. This chapter adopts this wider approach to governance. It focuses more specifically on two related issues:

- the problem of establishing who is responsible for doing what in the increasingly complex world of integrated service delivery; and
- developing structures and processes for ensuring accountability in circumstances in which responsibility is widely diffused.

The analysis complements the discussion in chapter two of the way in which citizens might be more fully engaged in the development and delivery of integrated public services. The closely connected issue of developing appropriate governance regimes for inter-jurisdictional service transformation initiatives is discussed in chapter five.

Background

This analysis starts from the premise that a fully realized, integrated and networked-based approach to service delivery is widely viewed to be a desirable outcome. This development is seen as an appropriate evolution from a pre-Internet world focusing on competition and customer to an increasingly online world emphasizing collaboration and integration. Collaboration stems from the tremendous opportunities for sharing information and integrating (or aligning) related service offerings across providers in different government ministries and agencies. The resulting networked architecture of service delivery, predicated on more seamless governance, is reflected in its earliest iteration as what the United Kingdom and other jurisdictions at times refer to as 'joined up' government (Batini et al. 2002; Bellamy, 6 Perri and Raab 2005; Scottish Executive 2006; Cross 2007).

This boundary spanning dimension of service transformation has fostered considerable intellectual ferment around the concept of the collaborative or network state. A recent Demos publication hails collaboration as the foundation for a new approach to delivering public services:

> It presents the possibility of replacing old rigidities with flexible federations of public bodies that can quickly sense and adapt to changing needs, at the same time creating new forums that bring people and institutions together to identify shared problems and work collaboratively on solutions (Parker and Gallagher 2007: 14).

To implement this vision, governments must collaborate internally from the top to bottom of organizations, as well as across agencies.

But the vision goes further than the stated goals of 'joined-up government' to call for collaboration with local service providers, private sector IT firms and service users in co-design and co-production. This type of thinking is fed by ideas and concepts from the 'wired' world and, more specifically, by the potential of Internet-based direct democracy and citizen-centred service delivery. By contrast with the NPM customer-oriented roots of service transformation, this more contemporary model of public administration is not market-oriented. Rather, it sees in the integration and alignment of services the opportunity to connect governments, private sector firms, community-based service providers and service users as citizens in the development and delivery of integrated services through more robust engagement and accountability relationships.

The network model recognizes the failure of traditional hierarchical government organizations to successfully deal with the complexity and interaction among many of the tough social and economic policy challenges facing societies, and the inability of individual agencies or governments to interconnect and reach out to wider community-based stakeholders (Considine and Lewis 2003). The network model also seeks to avoid the inefficiencies inherent in earlier efforts to reorganize government agencies into single large units by focusing on engaging existing agencies in joint problem solving without wasting time on reorganization or re-establishment of formal authorities (Goldsmith and Eggers 2004; Kettl 2005). This requires new forms of leadership and network management skills at all levels of government, substantial cultural change, and resource sharing arrangements and governance structures designed to support collaborative arrangements among public, private and not-for-profit agencies (Bakvis and Juillet 2004; Johnson 2005; Lindquist 2004).

All of this may be antithetical to parallel developments, such as the centralizing tendencies of the mainstream service integration movement; increasing government's control of not-for-profit service delivery agencies (Canada 2006a); the emerging power of IT firms in service delivery arrangements and, related to that, the increasing substitution of customer relations management for citizen engagement.

The shape of the collaborative governance challenge

Before exploring some shared governance experiences and setting out some responsibility and accountability principles to consider for the future, it would be useful to set out in a more orderly fashion the characteristics of these new service transformation initiatives that seem to call into question the effectiveness of traditional hierarchical approaches to governance. There are a number, and they all have to do with sharing responsibility for tasks that were traditionally performed by public servants working within one government organization ultimately responsible for the provision of the service.

First, there is the phenomenon of bundling or integrating public services provided by a number of different ministries or agencies within one government around larger user-defined problems or life events (Curtin, Sommer and Vis-Sommer 2003; Langford and Roy 2008b). This development within Westminster model governments breaks the simple accountability nexus focused on one responsible minister and officials in his or her ministry, recognizing instead the synergy of activities related to the desired public policy outcome (e.g., exporting, finding employment, etc.) performed by a 'joined-up' group of collaborating government agencies and ministers, none of whom can be held solely accountable either for the jointly sought outcome or how that outcome was accomplished (Bakvis and Juillet 2004; Lindquist 2004). Despite protests to the contrary, this shortcoming is not solved by simply establishing an integrating service organization (e.g., Service Canada, Service BC) where that agency is tasked to facilitate but not assimilate and control the activities of other public service delivery organizations.

Second is the particular need to seek long term partnerships with private sector IT firms to transform the related but separate face-to-face and phone-based service delivery systems into an integrated, multi-channel system making significant use of the Internet (Langford and Harrison 2001; Roy 2003; Langford and Roy 2006a). In most instances, these partnerships place enormous responsibility on the private sector IT vendor to recreate the front-end service-delivery system, to put in place back-office systems designed to accommodate the integration and, in many cases, to actually operate all or part of the delivery system, from call centres to billing operations.

Third is the parallel and more widely studied migration of service delivery responsibilities away from government organizations to non-profit and, less often, for-profit sector partners (Eggers 2005). This development similarly diffuses responsibility by diminishing direct control and potentially isolating ministers and officials from direct knowledge of outputs and outcomes (Kettl 2005; Van Slyke 2002).

Finally, the emergence of electronic government has disrupted the traditional control and oversight functions at the centre of government by encouraging the loosening of traditional procurement processes and introducing new players (e.g., chief information officers, partnership agencies, centralized service transformation or alternative service delivery secretariats, service delivery coordination organizations such as Service Canada, etc.) with different and sometimes competing control, oversight and accountability demands. Such organizations are added to (rather than replace) more traditional central agencies such as treasury boards, finance ministries and cabinet secretariats. This can create struggles for control of service transformation initiatives at the centre and have the effect of diffusing responsibility and the upward flow of accountability for service transformation initiatives in which online service delivery is a significant component (Kernaghan and Gunraj 2004).

In sum, our traditional ideal of democratic governance with reasonably clear establishment of responsibility, increasing degrees of transparency (at least after the fact) and an unbroken chain of upward accountability is severely challenged by these polycentric and network-based public service delivery initiatives, featuring multiple public service delivery organizations, new service integration agencies, a variety of private sector IT partners and, in many cases, further not-for-profit and private sector organizations contracted to deliver specific services. What then—in the context of our democratic traditions, public expectations and managerial capacities—would be a reasonable set of governance arrangements for a substantially more collaborative and boundary-crossing approach to service delivery? More specifically, what governance arrangements would best facilitate and sustain a workable sharing of responsibility and accountability?

How has this challenge been dealt with so far?

The continuing academic debate about public accountability in the parliamentary context has begun to take up these questions in recent years (Savoie 2004). Research on joined-up government in Westminster democracies has generated important observations and proposals for building accountability into horizontal collaborations among government agencies within and across jurisdictions (Considine 2002; Wilkins 2002; Ryan and Walsh 2004; Bakvis and Juillet 2004; Fox and Lenihan 2006). There are parallel streams of literature emerging about appropriate accountability arrangements in circumstances in which governments contract out existing service functions to non-profit sector agencies (Posner 2002; Goodin 2003; Canada 2006a); and completely privatize an activity (Hodge and Coghill 2004) and partner with private sector consortia to design, build and operate traditional public infrastructure such as bridges and hospitals (Hodge 2004; Flinders 2005). The issue of engaging service users as citizens in service transformation decision making and accountability processes has also begun to attract academic attention (Dutil, Langford and Roy 2007; Kernaghan 2008). However, there has been much less focused academic discussion of the potential governance paradigm shift that public-private IT service transformation partnerships might demand (Langford and Roy 2008a). Some of the most effective recent contributions to this particular debate have come from agencies such as chief information officers and audit offices (Australia 2004; Canada 2006b).

But progress on actually building new governance regimes for cross-boundary service integration in Canada has been more modest. Within individual governments, institutional governance arrangements for specific service transformation initiatives have often been quite informal involving, at most, some variation on an interdepartmental steering committee with representatives from the government agencies collaborating on the initiative in question. In some instances, more formal boards or authorities have been established, including all the government stakeholders and perhaps even non-governmental partners.

In recent years, the government side of the governance equation is becoming complicated by the creation of integrating service agencies (e.g., Service Canada, Service BC, etc.) tasked with implementing a whole-of-government or whole-of-policy area approach to service delivery. These organizations take a variety of forms; a small number are completely separate ministries or agencies (e.g., Service New Brunswick) while most others are effectively branches within ministries with wider mandates, often including shared services to government such as information technology, human resources management and procurement.

The advantages of creating a new governance entity—as opposed to less permanent forums or processes that link together representatives from the partner ministries—lies in the added flexibility to pursue innovation and process re-engineering. The logic is not unlike a government's decision to create a special agency or foundation empowered with more freedom than a typical line department. A new agency may also more readily facilitate the formation of innovative financing schemes. In such instances, the new agency is often identified by the opposition, media and even the government as the authority responsible for the success of the service transformation. In fact, our case studies suggest that these service agencies are often no more than a catalytic force in a more complex collaborative relationship with the traditional government service delivery organizations and the IT vendors. The underlying organization and funding for the delivery of government services in most cases, where new service agencies have been created, continues to be focused on the traditional service delivery departments or ministries, hamstringing the coordinating service agency in ways which further complicate accountability relationships.

In British Columbia, for instance, Service BC, located within the Ministry of Labour and Citizens' Services[1] was the driver of service transformation for some but not all service delivery ministries across the government. Broad service transformation visions and major initiatives may have been considered by a deputy ministers' council and/or approved by Cabinet, but actual service transformation initiatives were overseen by a cross-ministry committee of assistant deputy ministers. The committee had no formal government mandate but played a significant operational role in pushing forward both the service integration and multi-channel delivery strategies. Specific projects involving Service BC would be based on a service level agreement (SLA) among involved ministries and (most commonly) specific functional organizations (e.g., Enquiry BC, BC Online, etc.) within Service BC. A specific Service BC client manager would be tasked with working with the service managers from the involved line ministries who still retained complete responsibility through budget and legal mandate for the successful delivery of the service or services in question. These relationships were seen as client-based, with Service BC serving the needs of service ministry clients. In short, there is no formal institutional recognition that the responsibility for transforming a service or set of services is *collectively shared* and there are no formal mechanisms to hold managers or ministers *collectively accountable* for the success or failure of cross-ministry service transformation initiatives (Langford, MacDonald and Taschereau-Mamers, forthcoming).

With a few exceptions (one of which we will discuss later in this chapter), progress also seems limited when we examine the evolution of institutional design in the important service transformation partnerships between governments and major IT vendors (e.g., IBM, Sierra, Accenture, etc.).

Where the sharing of service delivery responsibility with IT vendors is limited to the outsourcing of carefully defined and largely repetitive tasks with clear performance standards (e.g., establishing and maintaining a website or call centre), the offence to the traditional public sector governance model is potentially containable. In such market-based relationships, suitable performance data might be produced to allow the ministry to report accurately on what was being done in its name by contracted agents. Penalty clauses can be invoked. Regular contract renewal negotiations can be used as a device to leverage learning. And, finally, independent auditing and user complaint offices can be employed to bridge the information and reporting divide between service users and the ultimately responsible government organization.

But when the relationship between the government and private sector IT partners slips from directive to collaborative and the model becomes network rather than market or hierarchically-based, the challenge to the traditional values of public sector governance becomes significantly more troubling. Increasingly, in the era of e-government and online service delivery, government service delivery agencies are becoming enmeshed in longer term, innovative, multi-channel service provision relationships with private sector IT firms or consortia of firms (Langford and Roy 2008a). In such arrangements, the responsibilities of each party can be difficult to clarify. It is becoming increasingly common for governments to engage potential partners in dialogues designed to establish the vision for the multi-channel service system that will emerge from the partnership. When a choice is made among potential partners, such relationships cannot rely solely on contract specifications since both parties contribute resources while facing separate and shared risks.

In any case, transparency can suffer because of the demands of private sector firms for secrecy around specific contractual conditions and price points. Outcomes and performance standards may be unclear and open to dialogue, negotiation and re-invention as the transformation process unfolds and technology changes (Ibid.). In such circumstances, it becomes difficult, if not impossible, to hold the private sector partners to account as separate agents in any meaningful manner on a quarterly or annual basis (OECD 2003; Brown 2006). Moreover, there is a risk that government organizations may become continuously dependent on the private sector players for the delivery of services as the latter takes control of front and/or back office functions essential to multi-channel service delivery (Gronlund 2002; Borins 2004).

This dependency and the accompanying hollowing out of the ranks of middle level managers can diminish the capacity of government organizations to understand what is being done in their name by their partners and, as important, reduces their capacity to enforce learning and consequences if shortfalls in service delivery become visible (Australia 2006). In addition, there is a tendency in the early stages of online service transformation to perceive the service user as a *customer*: a tendency which is reinforced by the importation into the public sector of customer relationship management tools from the private sector. As a result, as we saw in chapter two, the democratic accountability links to the user are weakened or ignored despite the widely-vaunted potential of e-government to strengthen the role of the user as a *citizen*.

Relations between governments and non-governmental partners are usually established by contract and service level agreements and the governance processes established are legalistic in character. Most collaborative governance arrangements with the large IT vendors participating in service transformation partnerships involve little more than procedural tinkering with the traditional hierarchical model in hopes that it can be adapted to the emerging world of networks and partnerships. Much of this tinkering is drawn from the literature and practice of project management, despite the reality that many service transformation partnerships are hardly projects since they are never really finished. Instead, they are long term or even permanent in the sense that they create arrangements from which it would be difficult for governments, ministries and even private sector partners to withdraw (Langford and Harrison 2001). In project management language, accountable, partnership-based service transformation initiatives would be built on a solid business case and risk analysis, which would be worked through with stakeholders (most prominently, those government ministries whose business lines are being incorporated into a newly integrated service package). Such initiatives would be entrusted to a 'senior responsible owner' and would establish a review schedule tied to gates, checkpoints or on/off ramps (at which point decisions would be made to stop or continue) and regular internal audits (United Kingdom 2006b).

Such procedural innovations are often little more than window dressing from an outcome perspective as they are not underpinned by a reliable performance measurement system, including elements such as: i) benchmarks; ii) specific outcome targets and deadlines; iii) accurate status reports and performance data related to quantifiable, objective and jointly agreed upon output and outcome indicators; iv) incentive arrangements with respect to reaching or exceeding targets; and v) the capacity to transform the partnership agreement to meet changing circumstances (Metzenbaum 2006). In addition, very few partnership arrangements contain a functioning governance structure based on the principles of open information sharing and joint decision making in which reliable information about performance problems is taken seriously.

The procedural innovations found in the project management framework also have other limitations. The opportunities that they provide for accounting are inherently bureaucratic and largely internal to the public sector partner. In other words, they tend to focus accountability on a senior public official in the service delivery agency and largely ignore this individual's counterparts among the various public and private partners. There is nothing 'shared' about such a system, which seems more designed to reduce the risk of government exposure than enhancing the jointly produced service. There is also nothing 'public' about such arrangements.

The assessments produced are managerial in character and rarely tested in a political or public forum unless an external auditor makes a special effort—usually in dire circumstances—to examine and publicize service transformation activities (Langford and Harrison 2001). These concerns echo similar shortcomings already noted in relationships among government agencies engaged in shared service transformation initiatives.

Unfortunately, as the reports of external auditors often make clear, useful outcome performance information is not regularly produced and when it is, it is often ignored. In general, there would appear to be little incentive within these complex service transformation partnerships to produce performance data for significant service delivery transformation initiatives. The most obvious and ubiquitous problem is that political leaders will be embarrassed by failures or setbacks. And there have been many costly failures on the IT side. But this is not the only reason for the lack of success in this area. Equally important is the absence of solid historical data against which to measure performance changes, especially in circumstances where the partnership is involved in a true transformation of the service provided (Cresswell, Burke and Pardo 2006).

In addition, as we are more generally aware, quantifiable service performance indicators (especially on the outcomes side) are hard to establish in government, and the skills and funds required to build and use measurement models are often in short supply. These factors combine too often to lead to the establishment of "timid targets, measurement manipulation, measurement elimination, outcome avoidance (resulting in an affinity for output targets) and claim games…" (Metzenbaum 2006: 6). Some authors even suggest that such antics may be part and parcel of an unspoken rationale for such entrepreneurial arrangements, namely the avoidance of normal government accountability processes (Moe 2001).

Rethinking the governance of service transformation

The future of service transformation lies in ambitious advances in service integration across ministries, governments and sectors. In this section we argue that for such innovations to work effectively and create trust among partners, stakeholders and citizens, they must be built on governance structures and processes which share power among partners appropriately; are reasonably transparent; and provide for levels and forms of accountability in line with our democratic values. Our limited review of present practices suggests that Canadian governments are a long way from meeting these criteria. In order to provoke further discussion about how to go about building defensible governance systems, we put forth five propositions with respect to the adaptation of the governance systems within which network-based service delivery arrangements are embedded.

1. Within and across jurisdictions, governance arrangements should recognize and clarify the different (but interlocking, interdependent and changing) roles and responsibilities of the network participants including service delivery ministries, facilitating agencies, IT partners, non-profit organizations and engaged central agencies.

Whatever the specific institutional arrangements, the responsibilities of the various players should be set out in the contractual arrangements with the IT vendors and non-profit agencies and memoranda of understanding among the various government participants. These documents (excluding precise commercial arrangements, perhaps) should be widely available.

At the central agency level, as noted, the roles and responsibilities of traditional bureaucratic agencies (treasury/management board, procurement agency) and more recently created players—such as the public-private partnership (P3) agency, chief information officer, central service transformation secretariats—need to be more clearly established in a manner recognizing both separateness and interdependence (Pardo and Dadayan 2006; Cross 2007).

2. It is reasonable that shared accountability should focus primarily on performance related to outcomes.

To many this proposition seems almost self-evident, since the very purpose of these multi-faceted partnerships is to add public value. Governments turn to partnerships among service delivery ministries, IT vendors and non-governmental service agencies because the latter ostensibly have potentially more sophisticated and cost-efficient ways of creating, maintaining and enhancing multi-channel delivery systems. Therefore assessing such partnerships on their outcomes is of primary importance (Moe 2001). As noted, the major issue with the focus on outcomes is the capacity of partnerships to jointly construct and maintain effective performance reporting, measuring and evaluation systems (Reed 2004). This challenge, of course, is not limited to the measurement of the performance of networked service delivery arrangements.

3. Accountability for performance related to process and how business is conducted cannot be ignored.

In many of these partnership arrangements, IT vendors and non-profit agencies actually provide the services, dealing directly with the service user. As these users are also citizens, then the way the vendors do their business (assess needs, establish wait times, deal with complaints, etc.) is also important. The service users will not necessarily understand the complexity of the service delivery arrangements, but they will still expect that the service operation "be fair, equitable, correct, timely, and not inadvertently disadvantage them" (Turner 2004: 133).

In addition, partnership arrangements can be open to patronage influences and conflicts of interest, especially in circumstances in which IT personnel and political aides cycle among ministers' offices, government service agencies, vendor firms and the consulting companies which often facilitate these partnerships. In such circumstances, Crompton suggests that the standard of process accountability levels be equal to those that would be applied to a service provided by the employees of a single government agency (Turner 2004).

4. There should be established boundary-spanning mechanisms for collective and joint information sharing, problem solving, decision making, learning, and recognition—both reward and punishment.

In most cases partnerships are truly joint ventures, bringing together the visions, skills and resources (including financial) of several parties. We may need strong hierarchical leadership within government to launch, frame and sustain collaborative service transformation ventures (Whitehead 2003), but such an arrangement will not work if one government partner, bowing to the traditional notion of sole accountability, tries to force its views and decisions on the other public sector and non-governmental partners and become the only accountability channel for the partnership. If the shared responsibility notion is taken seriously, then accountability at the political, management and operations levels of the partnership must be a joint activity (Dutil, Langford and Roy 2005; Lenihan 2007).

In such a structure, established and authoritative venues would be available for jointly planning, making decisions, considering performance feedback, updating targets and coordinating action plans and longer term strategies designed to deal with implementation shortfalls. There are a variety of studies setting out performance or public value measurement systems with the above features (Cresswell, Burke and Pardo 2006; Metzenbaum 2006).

5. Shared governance should have a public dimension.

There should be forums beyond joint managerial councils and operational meetings in which performance is discussed. This raises issues of transparency and access to information especially in the competitive world of IT firms where information about systems, software and price points is closely held (Barton 2006). Service integration partners have to be open to review by higher level bureaucratic bodies (e.g., departmental level committees, departmental and central agency level CIOs, Cabinet-level e-government units, etc.). The operations of a partnership must also be directly accessible to the review of the legislature (or legislatures, municipal councils, etc. in the case of multi-jurisdictional initiatives) at least through the activities of oversight committees and their agents (e.g., audit office, freedom of information and privacy commissioners, integrity officers, etc.), which report directly to the legislatures. Technical solutions have been proposed which would allow controlled access to relevant data bases by public and private auditors but such systems remain largely at the conceptual level (Turner 2004). The issue of whether public accountability processes in an adversarial political environment might be made more tolerant of the risks being taken by all parties to a partnership and, therefore, more willing to focus on learning and course correction is also open to question (Reed 2004).

Case study: A new shared accountability regime in British Columbia

To illustrate how this set of governance principles might be applied, we discuss them in the context of one aspect of the service transformation process in British Columbia: a partnership between Service BC and IBM designed to build a more effective multi-channel service delivery system for a number of transactional government services. This provides the reader with an opportunity both to consider the validity of the five propositions and to assess how well the notion of shared accountability has been incorporated into a recently established service transformation partnership agreement.

As noted, to facilitate integration and interoperability across government service delivery ministries and the development of refurbished IT capacities across a more holistic governance architecture of multiple and aligned delivery channels, the BC government created Service BC within the Ministry of Labour and Citizens' Services as the body responsible for leading service transformation on a government-wide scale. It also adopted a 'joint solutions procurement' process for the evaluation and selection of vendors in large IT projects. The process abandoned traditional tendering processes by engaging potential private sector partners in a multi-stage joint discovery of the risks and benefits of the proposed initiative and the capacity of the bidders to work with the government to create the desired service outcomes (ITAC 2004).

The Service BC–IBM Canada agreement

Following a 'joint solutions procurement' process that began in October 2004, the Province of British Columbia signed a master service agreement (MSA) in June 2005 with a private sector IT consortium led by IBM Canada.[2] In doing so, the BC government put forth the following objectives:

- integrate the telephone, online and in-person service channels to provide consistent information and services to its citizens;
- develop an approach to service channel management in which touch-points, technology platforms, data access and business processes are developed around the needs of the citizen; and
- more effectively meet the needs of its clients and customers within a new integrated, cost-effective and efficient service delivery environment.

The private consortium is thus called upon to provide a range of contact centre, portal and other service transformational services in order to foster this integrated multi-channel delivery framework. The agreement stipulates that all service delivery channels will be maintained (and improved), according to citizens and their choices of how to interact with government. A contractual guarantee of no job losses within government as a direct result of this agreement is also provided for. The base value of the contract is a modest CA$ 35 million over eight years. However, the partnership is structured in such a way as to augment the value to companies as service offerings expand over time. The MSA underpins specific gains-sharing arrangements through both efficiency savings and performance improvements, while IBM is similarly subject to financial penalties if service targets are not met.

The shared accountability regime of the Service BC–IBM partnership is anchored by the governance structure which provides a framework for jointly facilitating the achievement and monitoring of the partnership's objectives. The structure is a four-tiered arrangement establishing the roles and responsibilities for each partner at the operational, business and executive levels.

At the most senior level, 'executive sponsors' (the assistant deputy minister for Service BC and the vice-president for Business Consulting Services, IBM Canada) provide oversight of the relationship between the partners and the overall deal performance, and are the last level of escalation within the informal dispute resolution process. At the next level down, the Joint Executive Committee provides strategic direction and overall guidance to the executive sponsors in addressing issues such as scope, service levels, chronic failure, timeframes, budget allocations and stakeholder relations. At level three, the Service Integration Committee works to ensure operational success by providing advisory support and guidance to the Joint Executive Committee. This committee also addresses issues that impact scope, including changes to or additional statements of work; performance and service levels; resource sufficiency and availability; and change requests and change management issues. Finally, at the operational level, project teams are responsible for daily operations; emerging opportunities; workload and workload forecasting; issue management; and resolution for items within their specific operational mandates. There is no decision making authority at this level unless specifically delegated.

The issues dealt with by units of the governance structure originate at the operational and project level. Here, the broad objectives of the partnership are implemented in the form of projects run by teams comprised of staff from the province and IBM Canada. Service level targets and deadlines are assigned to these teams to which both government and IBM members are answerable—remedies for failure, however, are only outlined for IBM staff as failure on the part of public employees is an internal matter. The targets and deadlines are typically set out in the statement of work for each project area in the MSA, which provides a certain level of authority to enforce attainment of the stated goals.

Each level of the governance structure includes members of both parties, which provide a formal arrangement for shared planning and decision making. All decisions at each level must be made by mutual consensus of both government and IBM members. These decisions are binding and as long as they occur within the mandate of that governance level, there is no need to seek ratification from a higher level. When decisions are outside the authority of a particular governance level, there is a process of escalation up the structure to the appropriate level. Should the decision effect any significant change, a change order process is carried out.

Operating outside of the formal governance structure, but possessing considerable power in overseeing the progress of the partnership is the Business Office, comprised of Service BC and IBM staff, representing the primary management mechanism during the partnerships lifecycle. The business office is the official channel for communication between the partners and is responsible for building an effective working relationship. The business office also monitors the overall performance of the partnership and the results produced. It is responsible for contract management, program/project management, issue management and financial analysis. This includes overseeing project status reports and communicating and escalating problem alerts.

The reporting requirements for the partnership are outlined in the MSA. These requirements deal specifically with three categories. First, operational, project and transformational reports include the business requirements of the different areas of the partnership. The second focuses on compliance problems with respect to the privacy protection standards established for IBM and subcontractor employees. There are increasing sensitivities in this area especially in the context of concerns about the application of US *Patriot Act* provisions to confidential data held by subsidiaries of US firms. IBM Canada and its employees are under obligation to report any potential disclosure which might offend the privacy, security and confidentiality provisions of the province's freedom of information and privacy protection legislation. In addition, IBM employees must be made aware of obligations to report foreign demands for disclosure to a provincial government 'hotline'.

The third, and most strongly emphasized in the MSA, is reporting requirements related to service performance. An ongoing performance assessment strategy exists to monitor and evaluate the success of each project team in meeting service level targets and deadlines. Each IBM project team lead produces a bi-weekly status report, and project team leaders are then responsible for addressing significant performance shortfalls with the service integration committee. Serious issues will quickly make their way further up the governance structure for decisions concerning mutually agreed upon corrective action. All such reports are then brought into an integrative 'dashboard', a holistic performance assessment tool for both parties. Consolidated reporting through a quarterly balanced scorecard reviewed by senior managers from both partners also ensures both oversight and adjustment. IBM is primarily responsibility for creating and maintaining such reporting, and they are also obliged to support Service BC in responding to any requests for information made by central agencies.

The performance reporting system also provides tools for evaluating the performance of the partnership and initiating changes on an ongoing basis. Indicative of shared operational accountability, both Service BC and IBM may initiate a change order process. This is typically done through the business office but can also be initiated through the Service BC or IBM executive sponsor. These changes most often relate to a shift in the scope of the services described in the MSA and changes to service levels, and must be agreed to by both parties. A record of all changes is jointly maintained and incorporated into the overall operational change management process. If failure to achieve service levels is attributed to some failure on the part of IBM, the province does have recourse to terminate the specific statement of work and to revisit the MSA itself. In such cases IBM defaults any claim for payment (although financial liabilities are contingent on a joint determination of the reasons for the problems occurring).

A number of external oversight opportunities have also been built into the MSA. The province has extensive rights to perform audits, inspections and investigations related to matters such as privacy and security; general controls and procedures; financial and business matters; and gross margins. The province can use internal or external auditors and advisors and has the prerogative to apply this regime to both IBM Canada and its subcontractors. The provincial auditor has full access to the books of both partners.

The Service BC–IBM shared accountability regime and the five propositions

The governance provisions of the Service BC–IBM Canada partnership agreement reflect both the continuing influence of the business-oriented project management model and the acceptance of some key aspects of the shared accountability framework set out in section three.

The influence of the business model is strong. Born of a more flexible approach to the procurement of IT services, the partnership is intended to be a truly collaborative joint venture in which both parties commit resources to build an integrated service delivery system, the nature of which will evolve over the course of its development. The partnership is focused on results. The work is divided among project teams jointly staffed by the partners and tasked to achieve service level targets. The project teams have considerable flexibility for innovation in achieving targets. While there are no 'gateways' *per se*, the partnership is built around regular performance reporting up through a joint governance structure with the authority to informally solve problems and make the changes required to create a new service delivery system that works.

But the new partnership also shows some significant signs of developing a shared accountability system suitable for a system of democratic public administration. Referring to our five criteria: first, the partnership is grounded in a master service agreement which clearly establishes the roles and responsibilities of the two partners. Second, the MSA also lays out a four level, boundary spanning governance system with equal representation by both partners at all levels and a solid commitment to a consensus-based decision-making model. The governance system is focused on information sharing, learning and making decisions designed to solve problems and improve performance. The business office provides a significant level of joint oversight and control. Consequences for performance deficits are spelled out, at least for the private partner. Third, there is a strong focus on results and performance reporting at all levels. Fourth, there is an important, if narrowly focused, emphasis placed on process accountability, with the unique obligations on the private partner to monitor and report upon inappropriate access to personal data. Finally, there is also a significant public dimension to the accountability system, manifested most obviously in the inspection and investigation powers vested in the province and the complete access of ministry and provincial auditors to the activities and books of both partners.

Yet as progressive as it may appear on paper, this partnership arrangement does not entirely meet the test established in our joint accountability framework. The MSA itself is not a public document although a very detailed report on the contents of the agreement is available on the ministry website. Except for the references to auditors, the MSA does not establish the roles and responsibilities of government stakeholders outside the managerial structure of the ministry. The roles and potential power and influence of the deputy minister, minister, affected Cabinet colleagues (and their service delivery agencies) and key central agencies are nowhere formally spelled out. The performance reporting system is extensive, although the emphasis at the outset is most prominently on targets defined in terms of project outputs rather than on outcomes related to effective services to citizens. The focus on process accountability is very narrowly on privacy protection issues—a situation partially mitigated in this case by the fact that IBM employees are not interacting directly with service users.

What may be most striking, however, is the weakness of the fifth element of our framework—a public dimension to shared accountability. While there are opportunities for provincial monitoring agencies to investigate and report on the operations of the partnership, this is still an activity of government which will operate without the regular engagement of ministers, the legislature and the public. The reflex action on the part of many officials in government and industry is to argue that such issues are not inherently political—largely technical and operational in scope; they are best left to senior managers with only the broadest of oversight and direction-setting by elected officials. Yet, this explanation falls short. Political support and leadership have proved instrumental in the creation of partnership-based governance and in the orchestration of a government-wide service focus. The absence of a comprehensive public dimension to accountability in the BC model may become a serious drag on the sustained expansion of the service transformation architecture.

Conclusion

Successful collaborative or network governance is a key building block of service transformation. The BC case study suggests that it is possible to introduce strong joint accountability features into a contractually established governance regime for a service transformation partnership. We need to take more governance initiatives of this sort as part of service integration reforms if we hope to create effective partnerships and build public trust.

But, despite this interesting BC case, the prospects in Canada for shared accountability are far from positive. We rhetorically rally around the idea of shifting away from a model of hierarchical direct service delivery to one of networked government using a web of government agencies, and private sector and non-profit partners—the so-called value delivery network—to transform service delivery. But the cultural and managerial challenges to collaboration at the operational level (discussed in chapter three) are often accented by our ambivalent attitude towards this vision of joined-up governance. We profess to be devoted to collaboration but continue to support hierarchically-oriented goal setting, service planning, decision making, resourcing and monitoring systems that encourage isolation and competition rather than partnership. Building in shared accountability for outcomes is a particularly vexing governance challenge especially where the partnerships cross departmental, jurisdictional or sectoral boundaries. We find it hard, for instance, to imagine reshaping governance structures and processes to allow for joint reporting by public and private partners right up to the senior bureaucratic and political levels. But it is this kind of creative rethinking that will allow genuine boundary crossing service delivery to truly take root in our democratic governments.

Endnotes

1 The name was changed in 2009 to Ministry of Citizens' Services.
2 All of the subsequent information on the master service agreement (MSA) between the province and IBM Canada is based on: the *Service BC Project Summary Report*, June 2006; performance reports for 2007, 2008 and 2009 on the Service BC Project by the Alliance Management Office, Ministry of Labour and Citizens' Services; interviews with Ministry of Labour and Citizens' Services and IBM personnel conducted in spring 2007; and follow up interviews with the renamed Ministry of Citizens' Services personnel in spring 2010. While the accountability model spelled out in the MSA remains in place, the annual performance reports and follow up interviews provide no useful information on the implementation and operation of the governance provisions. Ministry officials interviewed in 2010 were unwilling to comment on any aspect of the governance relationship with IBM and IBM officials were also unwilling to be interviewed on the topic. This reticence appears to be related to ongoing negotiations related to the renewal of the master service agreement.

CHAPTER FIVE

Can We Work Across Jurisdictional Boundaries?

Service transformation transcends jurisdictional boundaries across levels of government. Whether the public is demanding a fully seamless public sector, for any given country, or even significant movement in this direction, is a more complex and contested notion (Turner 2004; Dutil, Langford and Roy 2007). Yet there is evidence to suggest that the public is demanding that governments work together more effectively (Heintzman and Marson 2005; Kernaghan 2005; Borins et al. 2007). In response, governments in Canada have begun acting in concert with one another to creative initiatives such as BizPaL (www.bizpal.ca), a common portal differentiated by community, designed to gather in a single location all services and regulatory requirements for the establishment of a new business enterprise.

Yet the potential for disappointment and confusion also exists. For example, BizPaL does not allow governments to share the information gathered across jurisdictional processes, and while there are some limited examples of such sharing (common business registration processes for example), service users are left to complete separate requirements via separate online systems (that may or may not be fully updated and integrated into the common BizPaL platform). Furthermore, service entities both federally and provincially often exist—with new dialogues emerging as to what relationship between these levels (and municipal equivalents such as 311 call centre systems) is both desirable and optimal.

The key design question in going forward thus becomes how to retain the benefits of federated models (either in a formally political sense or more administratively) while creating additional value for the citizen through more collaborative service delivery mechanisms where appropriate? A deceptively simple answer is to respect political jurisdictions while fostering integrative delivery mechanisms via either a single window (online or others), a set of service integrators, or ultimately a single service provider.

In order to better frame a path toward such a vision, a recent Crossing Boundaries National Council report on citizen-centric federalism provides a four-stage 'integrative continuum' meant to shift from the least to most complex of tasks: i) co-location of services; ii) streamlining services; iii) service policy alignment; and iv) collaborative governance arrangements for integrated services (Ambrose, Lenihan and Milloy 2006). It is important to stress that the heightened complexity of each stage cannot be viewed purely through the lens of administrative innovation. The third and fourth stages in particular are dependent on political innovation in putting in place new structures and new cultures suitable for an environment of interdependence and more networked governance patterns.

This chapter examines the tensions between political federalism on the one hand, and new and more integrative and cross-jurisdictional models of service delivery on the other hand. The former lens of inter-governmental relations emphasizes separateness and sovereignty (with a particular challenge for constitutionally subordinate municipalities), whereas the latter lens, as per the Crossing Boundaries vision, is one of political collaboration and administrative alignment through new governance mechanisms that are beginning to take shape in different parts of the world. This chapter thus draws from comparative examples in both unitary and federalism jurisdictions in order to examine the specific challenges confronting Canada in this regard.

Political federalism and service integration

One might assume that the technology-driven emphasis on service integration combined with the emerging, and related, notion of the network state and its collaborative relationships across all levels of government and into the wider community would bleed over into the political executive and scholarly thinking about federalism. In Canada, at least, this is not the case.

Federalism is a form of constitutional government that separates authority between the national government and provincial or state governments. This sharing of authority allows the accommodation of regional and cultural differences in a diverse nation. In some cases, such as in Switzerland, the state governments are more powerful than the national government. In

Canada, the national government tends to be more powerful than the provincial governments. In the United States, the center of power has swung back and forth over the decades.

Canadian federalism at the outset in 1867 was a reflection of the influence of the American experience on the authors of the Canadian Constitution. The sharing of state authority between central and provincial governments accommodated regional language and cultural interests already reflected in the existence of pre-Confederation governments. The intention of the framers may have been to create weak provincial governments, but over time, and particularly over the last half century, there has been a significant growth in the power of provincial governments and an increasing tendency for central and provincial governments to operate simultaneously in areas of jurisdiction that appear in the Constitution to be within the authority of one or the other levels of government.

As constitutional creatures of the provinces, increasingly economically important municipal governments have become frustrated participants in the contemporary intergovernmental mix. These developments and the concentration of financial power in the hands of the federal government have created complex power and resource sharing arrangements and placed an increasing premium on the need for more effective models of intergovernmental relations.

With very few exceptions (Ibid.), reflections on the development of federalism and intergovernmental relations in Canada remain focused on issues such as the shifting balance of power and fiscal resources among federal and provincial governments; the appropriate leadership role of the federal government; the limitations which should be placed on the federal government's spending power; the evolution of executive dominated federalism; and the capacity of the federal system to contain robust expressions of cultural, language or indigenous identity (Bakvis and Skogstad 2008). At the political level, contemporary debates on such issues have been focused on adjectives such as 'asymmetrical' and, more recently, 'open' federalism.

The conceptual flirtation with the notion of 'collaborative' political federalism, which began in Canada in the mid-1990s, recognizes the growing interdependence of federal, provincial, territorial and municipal governments and is in tune with the new public management (NPM) focus on decentralization and the development of more flexible, informal and equal arrangements among governments (Ibid.). But the discussion of collaborative federalism to date has focused largely on the co-determination (by the federal, provincial and, more recently, northern territorial governments) of broad national policies such as the Social Union Framework Agreement (SUFA) and the 1995 Agreement on Internal Trade (Cameron and Simeon 2002; McIntosh 2004).

Political leaders and federalism scholars have paid little more than lip service to the idea of extending the scope of the collaborative federalism model to include cross-boundary activities of service delivery agencies. This means that federal-provincial integrative initiatives such as the development of labour training agreements,[1] the efforts to create a cross-country health information network[2] and the more recent collaborative funding of infrastructure renewal[3] are happening largely outside of the political and academic debate about the future of federalism.[4] This continued focus within the mainstream federalism dialogue on traditional topics and high-level policy issues has resulted in a substantial disconnect between the citizen-centred service integration initiatives and networking activities at the bureaucratic, business and third sector level, on the one hand, and the focus of federalism scholars and more senior political and bureaucratic executive practitioners on the other.

The extension of the collaborative federalism model to embrace the world of cross-boundary service transformation would provide a platform for the marriage of thinking about the evolution of federalism to the emerging analysis of the network state and the intense 'underground' bureaucratic ferment among governments in Canada around cross-boundary service integration. Ambrose and others argue that adding the administrative dimension of service integration to the mix would have a positive impact on the management of higher policy issues dividing the country by deepening the economic and social union within the federation from the bottom up (Ambrose, Lenihan and Milloy 2006). There are further potential symbioses here as both streams of thinking focus attention on the extension of the inter-jurisdictional model to embrace not only provincial, territorial and local governments but First Nations governments and the growing web of non-state actors that either deliver many of the services in question as partners or contracting agencies of governments at all levels, or band together in stakeholder organizations representing service recipients.

This discussion is not designed to undermine the significance of political federalism in Canada or in other federations. Many historical rationales of federalism remain—geographic and linguistic diversities and a more operational belief that smaller, separate and more focused governments closer to their citizenries often yield stronger performance and accountability than a larger and more centralized governing model.

A look at models elsewhere

Countries around the world are struggling with such dynamics, with responses dependent on the starting point of the jurisdictional boundaries and how such boundaries are transcended (or not) by various coordinating mechanisms. In a unitary state model such as Denmark, for example, multiple levels of government co-exist in an environment viewed by both the public and governments themselves as interrelated components of a single system. This sort of starting point is therefore more conducive to charting a collaborative, integrative course based upon more seamless governance architecture. Danish e-government and service transformation efforts have long featured, since their inception, formal inter-governmental planning and coordinating mechanisms to proceed in this manner—other Nordic countries are similar in this regard, as is the Dutch model (Langford and Roy 2008b).

Belgium is perhaps the world's poster child for inter-jurisdictional complexity. Prior to recent elections (leading to an extended episode of political paralysis), one national newspaper published a series of articles over several days in a valiant effort to explain to readers the intricacies of electoral processes across federal, regional and linguistic community-based legislatures. A strong effort has been made over the past two decades to improve administrative alignment and coordination across various levels of government. A turning point in this regard came in 2001 when a formal cooperation agreement was signed between the federal government, the regions, and the communities to forge a common platform for electronic service delivery (Ibid.).

Building on this common platform, in 2003 Belgium became the first European country to launch a national electronic ID card, an exercise that began with a federally-sponsored pilot in several municipalities before proceeding to national rollout. The card includes a unique identifier for each citizen that is now enabling electronic data exchanges and service provisions across widening segments of the county's social security and health care systems. A critical aspect of this identity management system is the Crossroads Bank for Social Security (CBSS), an autonomous public sector body whose origins date back to 1990 when it was established to form an initial repository for information holdings for citizens and employers contributing to or benefiting from social security programs. Accountable to a management board with representatives of the public, companies and government service providers, today the CBSS works as a 'service integrator' for all Belgian federal social security benefits and the integration of these benefits with services provided by other government levels.

The Belgian federated approach is seemingly intent on not allowing political separateness (and corresponding democratic accountabilities) to stymie a more networked and integrative approach to the organization and management of service delivery. The ability to do so is owed in no small measure to two central elements: first, the willingness of all governments in the Belgian context to formalize a collaborative framework early on; and second, the common infrastructure provided by CBSS to the country's public sector as a whole (Ibid.).

National frameworks versus local innovation

Transformative e-government implies an extension of the collaborative logic of federated architectures, integrated service delivery, and more participative governance mechanisms beyond the boundaries of any single government. A particular challenge in this regard is that, while enterprise architecture and service innovation are often perceived to be primarily the purview of national governments, democratic experimentation with new technologies is being primarily driven by sub-national governments.

Electronic voting (e-voting), for example, was first adopted by the Swiss canton of Geneva and although few countries have adopted e-voting in a comprehensive manner, usage continues to expand at the local level in many parts of the world. Whereas many national governments, larger and more bureaucratically entrenched, face wider barriers to systemic innovation and change, more nimble governments at sub-national levels are often better able to embrace collaboration and change. There is little reason, then, as to why the collaborative logic of transformative e-government would not transcend jurisdictional boundaries—not only across government levels but between multiple government units at a particular territorial level.

One such example of shared capacities is the vision of "integrated Buckinghamshire where county and district councils see themselves as part of a coherent public service provision whilst retaining their local democratic strength and decision-making on policies and priorities" (United Kingdom 2007: foreword). A joint improvement board encompasses representatives of the area's five councils (four local-tier districts and one upper-tier county) in order to foster an integrative approach to citizen service and community engagement for the area's nearly half a million residents that includes:

- an integrated office of house approach to simplify contact for customers;
- integrated frontline service provision where this can deliver improvements and cost savings;
- use of joint procurement to drive down costs;
- joining of back office services where this can produce savings and a better service;
- integrated community engagement within an agreed framework at the local level; and
- a rationalization of consultation to avoid duplication, confusion and cost (Ibid.).

The initiative is thus notable for extending beyond what is becoming an increasingly common approach to shared services in back office functions and embracing a more integrated architecture to the front as well. Furthermore, the last point underscores the necessity of viewing service architecture and provision within the broader context of community engagement and two-way relationships between the public and their governments.[5] Although not as yet deployed in such efforts, elected and appointed officials leading this shared and integrative services strategy (and community engagement dimension in particular) are seeking to deploy social networking tools and online forums in order to further augment public awareness and discussion as initiatives progress—arguably a collective learning prerequisite to deeper forms of collaboration as public awareness and support translates into more direct buy-in by elected officials at the district and county levels.

Local officials point to the necessity of keeping partners engaged and satisfied, and identifying and achieving win-win outcomes as the largest and most important objective in making such an initiative work well. It is fully expected that as such collaborative opportunities are forged, one or more partners may choose to opt out of specific arrangements if unconvinced of the net benefit (though at present, more than a year into this pathfinder initiative, almost all working committees include participation from all five authorities). In a manner reflective of the service ecosystem logic, the new partnerships between local governments will also be enjoined in new public-private arrangements as well, specifically for the formation of a back-office, shared-services provider where the outsourcing of the provision of such services to a joint public-private venture is one of the leading options under consideration.

As underscored by the most recent United Nations Global E-Government Survey, it is often smaller jurisdictions such as the Nordic countries and Singapore that lead most rankings of e-government success. Indeed, even in larger, federated countries it is not unimportant in such matters that much of public sector innovation and reform continues to be an emergent process—with national reforms shaped by innovations benefiting from the flexibility and nimbleness of smaller, sub-national governments (Goldsmith and Eggers 2004; Stoker 2006; Langford and Roy 2008b).

Both integrated service delivery efforts aimed at an external user audience and shared service strategies for internal clients (i.e., departments and agencies) feature many similar governance challenges of collaborating across boundaries (both within and across various jurisdictional levels). This widening need for horizontality and intra-governmental networking is a key aspect of a more complex and less hierarchical public sector model and mindset—important in order for government to both help orchestrate the formation of and contribute to innovative service ecosystems. Much as external service providers face pressures and opportunities for wider engagement with service users and partners in devising innovative strategies (and learning from present and pending experience), a similar logic would apply to a shared services environment internally.

Rather than impose common infrastructure such as IT platforms and software programs on departments and agencies through centralized mechanisms of planning (often driven almost exclusively by efficiency objectives), a more inclusive and consultative approach is necessary in order to forge collaborative business models and shared accountability mechanisms (Belanger, Coe and Roy 2007). In doing so, participative Web 2.0 tools such as wikis and blogs and shared knowledge platforms can be crucial enablers of both creating new and more flexible mechanisms and constant adaptation to an ever changing environment.

Furthermore, with respect to collective intelligence, the creation of public value, an additional important lesson of this section, is that local governments may benefit from a more modest scale of activity and closer proximity to the public, augmenting the ability for governments to foster a more holistic dialogue with the public on new service arrangements both within and outside of public sector bodies (as well as the need for new governance mechanisms enjoining them). At the same time, with an increasingly well informed and virtual citizenry less tolerant of traditional inter-jurisdictional barriers (either formally in political federations or less formally), the need for holistic approaches to dialogue and public engagement for the public sector as a whole will only grow in importance. How such tensions are resolved will vary considerably across jurisdictions according to tradition and structure, but the fundamental point is the need to begin thinking holistically about both the technological and decision-making architectures of the public sector as a whole from a citizen-centric perspective.

Four challenges for Canada's public sector

A new, more aligned and integrative cross-boundary service model for a country as a whole is truly a transformative agenda that requires a holistic prism. Complex matters of governance, knowledge and people all come into play and, in a democratic context, politics cannot be absent from any such list. The commonality across these matters is an evolving thematic challenge for national and sub-national governments in Canada and elsewhere to collectively navigate an environment of growing interdependence across both policy and service realms. A good deal of bureaucratic experimentation is now underway in many developed countries, with considerable promise for the future. Yet the realization of such promise depends on far more than technology.

To illustrate this point, we set out five challenges which Canadian governments are facing, and we expect are facing governments in many other countries.

Challenge 1: Creating a common infrastructure
The primary connotation of the term service-oriented architecture (SOA) has typically been technological, in terms of forging interoperable electronic systems as enablers of customer or citizen-centric service delivery. Many strategists, however, would argue for a wider application of the term to include the alignment of technology and information management planning within a business model perspective of transformational change.[6]

Fluid and constantly shifting terminology notwithstanding, the need for common infrastructure has been a key horizontal driver both within and across governments, very much at the nexus of e-government and service transformation. In the late 1990s, the recognition of this need in Canada spawned two federal councils, the Public Sector Service Delivery Council (PSSDC) and the Public Sector Chief Information Officer Council (PSCIOC). A secretariat, the Institute for Citizen-Centred Service (ICCS), was created to support both councils through promotion of service transformation and research.

These councils were made up of representatives from federal, provincial and territorial governments; only some of the fourteen governments also funded the ICCS. The mandates of the councils were to foster improved public service delivery to Canadians through collaboration, information sharing and leadership across governments in service transformation and related information management and technology. These councils and the institute represent the highest expression of what we earlier described as a quiet cross-jurisdictional bureaucratic collaborative federalism.

Further evidence of the informal build-up of pressure for a common infrastructure has been a growing list of bilateral and multilateral cross-jurisdictional initiatives aimed at either sharing or integrating information including: portals for such client groups as senior citizens;[7] business registration via BizPaL[8] and Business Registration Online;[9] and vital events information sharing including the newborn registration service launched by ServiceOntario and Service Canada that provides quick and seamless access to parents for birth registration, birth certificates and social insurance numbers.[10]

As standalone initiatives, they are important examples of cross-jurisdictional service integration. The stumbling block emerges in attempting to stitch a number of these like-minded innovations into a broader quilt (or architecture) for systemic information management and business model planning across the public sector as a whole. One illustration of this is the recently-revived eContact initiative—a collaborative effort between federal and provincial governments designed to create a national repository of service standards and shared modeling for more interoperability (Moule 2007).

Many past struggles of eContact are attributable to the limited ties across jurisdictions and the difficulties of sustaining and expanding joint initiatives. An important lesson from other jurisdictions such as Belgium and Denmark is that although informal cooperation (of the sort provided by the federal councils) is a useful beginning, it cannot suffice in creating a more systemic approach to identifying opportunities and pursuing these opportunities through joint undertakings.

A greater level of formality is required, within which strategies and mechanisms must be resourced and empowered to pursue shared aims. The need for such formalization explains the emergence of bilateral arrangements such as the recent protocol on public sector renewal signed by the respective heads of the Governments of Canada and Ontario. With respect to service delivery both governments have committed to:

- expanding collaboration in citizen/business facing services;
- forging a common information technology infrastructure/backbone;
- establishing a protocol on the exchange of protected/sensitive information;
- exploring possibilities for service integration; and
- improving relationships with third party agencies (Ibid., 4, schedule A).

The importance of this agreement lies in the offering of an explicit layer of high-level support within which collaborative opportunities may be pursued. Nonetheless, Service Canada and ServiceOntario now face the important challenge of operationalizing such support into innovation, a step requiring not only interoperable electronic infrastructures but also at least partially integrated organizational infrastructures as well.

The challenge lies in the sorts of governance capacities required to move toward this integrative vision. Many early initiatives, such as eContact and shared research agendas, lie somewhere between 'cooperation' and 'collaboration'. Although the two words are often used interchangeably, distinguishing between them can also help underscore the different sort of expectations and commitment at play:

- *Cooperation.* Informal relationships that exist without any commonly defined mission, structure or planning; and
- *Collaboration.* A more durable and pervasive relationship involving shared structures and joint authority, a full commitment to a common mission and pooled resources, risks and rewards (Langford and Roy 2008a).

Moving toward a collaborative mindset and a common infrastructure requires a level of trust across jurisdictional boundaries acknowledged to be lacking at present (Entwistle and Martin 2005). The PSSDC lays out the issue well:

Trust continues to be a significant problem...public sector organizations as service providers still struggle to trust one another. As such, even if Canadians were perfectly prepared to give governments permission to use and share personal information for the purpose of identification, the goal of integrated, seamless service cannot be met until service organizations establish a level of trust between themselves (Public Sector Service Delivery Council 2006: 9).

Challenge 2: Agreeing on an identity management system

Identity management in Canada today lies at the crossroads between two approaches: either a loose, cooperative framework for sharing information and aligning solutions across otherwise separate jurisdictional systems; or a set of truly collaborative governance mechanisms underpinned by integrative capacities for decision making. The decision as to which route to take will be consequential in shaping inter-jurisdictional service capacities. As such it deserves further examination.

The need for an appropriate governance model to underpin any inter-jurisdictional framework for identity authentication and management has been well articulated in Canada by the recent PSSDC-housed Inter-jurisdictional Identity Management and Authentication Task Force (IATF 2007). Three models of inter-jurisdictional governance arrangements are presented as worthy of consideration by this task force's report, varied in structure but common in their formalized approach to collaboration:

- The *Canadian Council of Motor Transport Administrators*,[11] a non-profit corporation reporting to a council of ministers, supported by a secretariat and deputy minister council, and overseen by a board of federal, provincial and territorial senior officials;
- The *Ministerial Council on Social Policy Renewal*, supported by inter-governmental subcommittees and cross-sectoral councils;
- The *Canada Health Infoway*,[12] a non-profit corporation jointly accountable to federal and provincial governments with a board comprised of two federal appointees (including the chair), five provincial/territorial appointees, and six directors elected by members (who are the fourteen federal, provincial and territorial deputy ministers of health) (Ibid.).

These models all underscore that the aforementioned cooperative path is insufficient for a genuinely cross-jurisdictional system of identity management. A further basis of collaboration is required if more seamless service delivery mechanisms for the public sector as a whole are to emerge.

Following a meeting of federal, provincial and territorial deputy ministers with service delivery responsibilities held in late 2007, a decision was made to endorse the formal pursuit of a pan-Canadian framework for identity authentication and management. In 2008 a formal governance body, funding model, and work plan were agreed to by 'deputies'. One important rationale for a pan-Canadian approach to identity management is to ensure some level of technological commonality across jurisdictions—provincially and locally. As such, it is important that discussions pertaining to governance models for identity management systems and other aspects of inter-jurisdictional collaboration that may be required are situated in a broader dialogue on how the country's holistic approach to service models may also impact the broader developmental capacities for communities—the basis of the next challenge.

Challenge 3: Engaging citizens and communities in design and delivery

Much of the current discussion pertaining to information and identity as elements of cross-jurisdictional service innovation is first and foremost concerned with strategies and mechanisms for the delivery of public services. Increasingly, however, advocates of the network state insist that governments think and act more creatively about the design of public services, both within and across jurisdictions.

Although governments are no doubt devoting much time and energy to design matters, much of this activity happens from the inside looking out. Client segmentation and user surveys focus on the public as the user—a *de facto* customer primarily interested in transactional outcomes as opposed to citizen engagement. Such a view is increasingly being challenged as incomplete, both conceptually and practically, in jurisdictions such as Scotland.

In line with the emergence of a more participative paradigm for democratic governance and service design, performance is shared by resilience and capacities for learning and adaptation across the 'service ecosystem':

> In this new ecosystem model, leading governments also delegate service accountability to the relevant community for a new ability to drive outcomes. Local and municipal governments in turn take the chance to tailor what they do for the particular citizens that live there, leading to new thinking about delivering services not just to individuals, but also to families and communities (Accenture 2007: 8).

This challenge applies to all government levels, especially in federal countries such as Canada and Australia where federal service delivery actors play important roles in both individual and community development.

Yet it is precisely the nature of such 'roles' that requires a broader conversation not only among governments themselves but also across a broader range of stakeholders as well as with the citizenry. The sort of conversation required will need to be structured around questions and issues such as:

- public expectations about service integration across jurisdictions and how such expectations may vary across different sorts of communities (i.e., urban and rural, northern and remote, First Nations etc.);
- the appropriate balance between a municipal, provincial and federal presence at the interface between the public sector and the citizenry (and again, how this balance may not be uniform across the country in terms of both present conditions and future prospects and demands); and
- linkages between demography, geography and technology in not only shaping a community as a passive recipient of services but also a strategic partner in determining how delivery processes can contribute to policy and development objectives.

This latter point is a crucial aspect of the present emphasis on a new relationship between policy and service (both separating them via specialized service providers and integrating them by making good use of the knowledge gathered at the front line by these providers). Already complex with large organizational apparatuses provincially and federally, this relationship is bound to be more so across jurisdictions—but also more consequential in shaping developmental capacities across communities of varying size and intensity.

A good example of devolving service integration in this manner can be found in Canada's Northwest Territories where an innovative partnership model among the Dogrib Aboriginal communities, their own regional services authority and the territorial government. The new governance arrangement won a United Nations Public Service Award in June 2007.[13]

Service design therefore means not only gauging the public as to their immediate levels of satisfaction with existing encounters, but also engaging them in a dialogue about what sorts of services are most required, and how the selection and crafting of delivery mechanisms can improve community prospects for innovation and growth. Such a participatory approach is particularly essential for evolving multi-channel strategies and the public interest and collective trade-offs between matters, efficiency, employment and equity.

Whether it is identity authentication or public engagement for service design, the resulting imperative for inter-jurisdictional governance is a more collaborative mindset focused on community learning and performance (Woodward 2003).

Furthermore, the term 'community' need not be exclusively defined in territorial terms. The service delivery ecosystem, for example, implies a stakeholder community both within and outside of governmental confines—often transcending any specific locality. The result is the formation of new communities of practice across and between governments that are by definition non-hierarchical and more networked.

Challenge 4: Supporting network-based governance

Collaborative mechanisms for service integration must be built upon common informational architectures, but they are more fundamentally about ensuring the capacity to transform this information into shared decisions and integrative and better outcomes.

This shift in mindset is not an easy one to make. The distinction between information and knowledge is one aspect of this shift, with some commentators characterizing the latter as 'information in action' (MacDonald and MacDonald 2003). The knowledge management challenge in a networked environment is thus closely intertwined with governance in terms of the need for formalized structures and supportive cultures that enable different stakeholders to work together in flexible and innovative manners in pursuit of agreed upon objectives.

Experiences within specific jurisdictions can help shed light on this challenge (while also underlining the daunting scope of the required shift). For instance, one recent review of horizontal initiatives at the federal level in Canada highlighted the need to largely abandon command and control approaches that typically attempt to ordain change in a predetermined manner. By contrast, participation, consultation, and supportive and enabling frameworks are required:

> ...a management culture that relies less on command and control and more on financial incentives, continual monitoring, and ongoing consultation and engagement. Performance reviews and agreements that more explicitly capture the need to work horizontally could also go some way toward initiating a cultural shift (Bakvis and Juillet 2004: 14).

The absence of such a culture not only severely constrained many federal Government On-Line pathfinder projects meant to integrate services across departments, it is also proving to be consequential in ongoing uncertainty about the formal mandate and governance regime of Service Canada—and by extension, its collaborative capacities across the federal apparatus. As the formation of these sorts of partnerships and networks evolve across multiple organizations and jurisdictions, the governance dynamics become more complex and more collaboratively intense.

Conceptually, the essential elements of successful collaborative networks have been well identified:

- Members must see themselves as only one piece of the total picture. This requires seeing the points of convergence, not just those of contention. It also means that power must be shared or lost.
- Recognition that building relationships, not accomplishing tasks, is the primary goal in a network, since the task cannot be accomplished without the relationships, and the relationships will outlive any one task that the network might be called upon to address.
- Building relationships requires building trust and breaking down communications barriers that might exist between the members.
- Being able to listen to others rather than merely telling them what to do. This is linked to the ability to build on the different types of expertise available in the network rather than assuming that only you have the expertise needed to make a difference.
- Allow enough time and flexibility to give everyone the opportunity to make a difference. Traditional timelines and roles of authority will not allow for the risks that must be taken in order to develop relationships which will be the basis for establishing innovative solutions.
- Be able to make mutual adjustments, build coalitions and mobilize support in order to make things happen. Working in a network means that each member recognizes their interdependence and learns how to capitalize on their interdependencies (Mandell 2005).

Practically, realizing these conditions and translating them into results is a much harder undertaking to achieve—although a growing body of examples is becoming available for study due to the widening usage of networked strategies in today's environment (Agranoff 2003; Reed 2004; Milward and Provan 2006; Treadwell 2007). With respect to networked service delivery in Canada, one recognized example is the Southern Alberta Child and Youth Network, an initiative whose efforts are entirely dependent on the commitment and collective action capacities of member stakeholders.

According to the website, the network's two primary objectives are to: "develop and adopt a shared vision and purpose", and "identify and create opportunities for positive change in service delivery". A formal evaluation of the efforts of this network demonstrates tangible results that could only have been achieved in a collaborative manner while also underscoring the relevance and importance of many of the elements of networked leadership presented above (Alberta 2005).

The message for governments is that holistic transformation requires embracing a collaborative mindset in order to realize more seamless service delivery models encompassing multiple public sector bodies and jurisdictions. As the scope of networking expands so too does demand for workers who can function in an increasingly fluid and complex organizational context.

A global survey conducted by the Economist Intelligence Unit, in association with KPMG, is one of many such efforts to articulate the prototype of the future public servant as someone able to navigate complexity both internally and externally. In terms of roles perceived by public sector executives as destined to be most essential in 2020, two areas garnered the most support (62 percent and 32 percent, respectively) by a wide margin (Economist Intelligence Unit 2006):

- Complex knowledge-based roles that are primarily outward-facing and require developed communication and judgment skills; and
- Complex knowledge-based roles that are primarily inward-looking and require developed communication and inward looking skills (Ibid., 64).

For more holistic and integrative cross-jurisdictional models to take hold, this 'outward facing' dimension to collaborative governance between governments becomes essential. There is a need to extend the logic of the Service New Brunswick examples earlier to arrangements between or among governments—including site touring, informal conversation, joint discovery and shared action. These sorts of processes require high level support frameworks, but the essence of such an approach is more bottom-up and transversal, requiring both individual and organizational competencies that support experimentation and learning.

Smaller jurisdictions, whether provincial, territorial or municipal, carry both important assets and handicaps in terms of recruiting and nurturing the requisite levels of human capital necessary. Few resources is clearly a potential constraint but one that can be overcome by horizontal initiatives across jurisdictions (regionally, encompassing either municipalities or provinces, such as Atlantic Canada). It bears noting that much of public sector innovation and reform continues to be an emergent process—with national reforms shaped by innovations benefiting from the flexibility and nimbleness of smaller, sub-national governments (Goldsmith and Eggers 2004; Stoker 2004; Roy 2006a).

Conclusion: fostering a mindset of interdependence

We have thus far examined the opportunities and challenges associated with recasting inter-jurisdictional service transformation in Canada away from the existing cooperative, bureaucratic and experimental mode. Instead, what is increasingly apparent is the need for a more holistic, inclusive, collaborative and interdependent framework. Only then can the demands of citizen-centred service integration across jurisdictional boundaries trump the sorts of political and operational constraints imposed by a divisive and combative federal system.

Learning from other jurisdictions can help in order to gain insight into how governments in Canada can collectively address the challenges of integrated service delivery. At the same time, however, a genuinely collaborative and made-in-Canada approach is required—one that should be nurtured as much through bottom-up leadership and community engagement as from federal government leadership and action.

An encouraging sign has been the formation of a more formal working group of federal, provincial and territorial deputy ministers with service delivery responsibilities. The creation of such a body has already resulted in a greater impetus for more collaborative governance in the realm of identity management, a key foundational component of a more seamless public sector service delivery system. This group is an important complement to the work of the two inter-jurisdictional councils (PSCIOC and PSSDC) that also comprise municipal representatives as well.

Such efforts denote the contours of a new approach to federalism that is more in tune with an era of interdependence and seamless governance arrangements in both the service delivery and policy-making realms. Through these mechanisms and through greater interaction and dialogue, a more collaborative mindset should be pursued through such joint initiatives as:

- expanding knowledge repositories of critically analyzed and shared lessons and experiences from within jurisdictions;
- pursuing joint ventures in public sector training and professional development, both online and offline;
- fostering ongoing discursive mechanisms interlinking service providers at all government levels;
- investing resources to both stimulate and reward collaborative pathfinder projects that innovatively and meaningfully transcend jurisdictional silos;
- expanding opportunities for employee exchange and rotational assignments across government levels; and
- undertaking shared consultative efforts within specific localities and regions in order to engage the public as both a service recipient and stakeholder in service design.

Ultimately, embracing interdependence and the building of collaborative governance systems begin with dialogue (Yankelovich 1999). In a democratic context, politicians are the linchpin between the organization of public services and the citizenry, while also providing the mandate to proceed with change. Many illustrations of the importance of political leadership in collaborative service innovation across jurisdictions include:

- the political foresight by Belgian politicians to create the Crossroads Bank for Social Security in the very early days of e-government, while also forging agreement for a genuinely federated strategy inclusive of all jurisdictions;
- the Danish commitment to inter-governmental planning in balancing national interoperability and online channels with strengthened frontline municipal capacities;
- the Scottish focus on service transformation as a political priority for the newly devolved administration;
- the catalytic role of local elected officials across multiple districts and counties in the United Kingdom's Buckinghamshire region in

forging an integrative service model to transcend back office and front office divisions; and

- the ability of Australia's Centrelink to align its federal integrationist duties with a community partnering role to establish agency autonomy coupled with direct political oversight and leadership (Langford and Roy 2008b).

Despite strong federal leadership early on in the formation of the 1990s Connecting Canadians agenda, the 2007 global survey of government service delivery efforts completed by Accenture Consulting underscores the risk of political complacency as an area of concern for the Government of Canada—a risk highlighted several years ago by the Government On-Line External Advisory Panel in recommending Prime Ministerial ownership of the agenda.

The realization of integrative service models provincially has required commitment from senior politicians—a precursor to not only creating new service vehicles and empowering them with mandate and means, but also to sustaining efforts to overcome what can often be entrenched resistance to change. Similarly, the city of Calgary became Canada's 311 pioneer through a strong commitment by the mayor and the active involvement of elected officials in the design and implementation of this new service model (Dutil, Langford and Roy 2005).

The difficulties of instigating a national political discourse across jurisdictions, in a country arguably 'obsessed' with federal-provincial squabbles, are well known and widely acknowledged (Andrew 2002). Furthermore, concerns about local governance capacities are not new (OECD 2002; Paquet and Roy 2004; Gibbons 2004). Nevertheless, in health care, where fiscal and policy tensions often run high, innovations such as the Canada Health Infoway have emerged. In numerous other policy fields and agendas, moreover, concerted action between governments has contributed significantly to both stability and prosperity.

There are nonetheless limits to what can be accomplished without the structural change that only senior political leaders can sanction. The reluctance of politicians in Canada to embrace identity management as a political issue, as so many other jurisdictions have done, is a serious impediment to moving forward with a genuinely collaborative inter-jurisdictional service agenda. The risk of a widening gap between public expectations and performance results is real. Consequently, the need for governments to embrace a mindset of interdependence is growing in order to chart a holistic vision of service transformation for a country as a whole.

Endnotes

1 See, for example, the 2005 bilateral agreement between Ontario and Canada: www.edu.gov.on.ca/eng/training/labourmarket.html.
2 See *2015: Advancing Canada's Next Generation of Healthcare*, www.infoway-inforoute.ca/en/pdf/Vision_2015_Advancing_Canadas_next_generation_of_healthcare.pdf.
3 See *Building Canada - Modern Infrastructure for a Strong Canada*, www.building-canada-chantierscanada.gc.ca/plandocs/booklet-livret/booklet-livret-eng.html.
4 Such developments receive very brief recognition in: Johns, C. M., P. L. O'Reilly and G. J. Inwood 2007. "Formal and Informal Dimensions of Intergovernmental Administrative Relations in Canada."
5 With respect to municipal service innovation, the UK government has been aggressively promoting interoperable networks and standards across a common infrastructure for local authorities in both Scotland and England (and Wales). The UK Department for Communities and Local Government has funded the Government Connects initiative, providing a common platform for shared services and customer service initiatives.
6 See several articles in the July-August 2007 issue of *CIO Government Review*, www.itworldcanada.com/publication/CIO%20Gov.%20Review.htm.
7 See www.seniorsinfo.ca/
8 See http://bizpal.ca/index_e.shtml
9 See www.businessregistration.gc.ca.
10 See www.serviceontario.ca/newborn.
11 See www.ccmta.ca/english.
12 See www.infoway-inforoute.ca.
13 In the early 1990s there was increasing concern among the people and the leadership about health and social services provided by the government. They were often not culturally relevant and they did not seem to improve the lives of people in the communities. The leaders decided they wanted to take over these services. But they had a problem. They lacked people with expertise to serve on boards and fill staff positions, especially at the administrative level. Being very practical people, they came up with a practical solution. They decided to merge these new services with something they did know something about—how to run their own schools.

   In 1997 the GNWT and the Dogrib leadership signed an agreement to create the Dogrib Community Services Board. As a result of this agreement the GNWT transferred to the Dogrib the responsibility for managing:

   • Education services (schools, daycares, services for children with special needs and student residences);
   • Primary health care, (treatment and emergency services, the complete range of public health services, home support programs, dental therapy); and

- Child and family services, (child protection, foster care, community mental health, residential care and services for the elderly and handicapped).

On August 4, 2005, with the Tlicho Agreement, the Dogrib Community Services Board became the Tlicho Community Services Agency [TCSA]. It became an agency of the Tlicho Government and is now in the position to assume even more responsibility for services. The Partnership between the TCSA and the GNWT for service delivery is guided by the Tlicho Intergovernmental Services Agreement (ISA) between the Tlicho Government, on the one hand, and the GNWT and the Government of Canada on the other hand. It is the only such agreement in the Northwest Territories and distinguishes the relationship the Dogrib have with the GNWT and federal government from other relationships with regional boards. See www.tlicho.ca/services-agency/history.htm.

CHAPTER SIX

Will Web 2.0 Change Everything?

Over the past decade service transformation and e-government have been closely intertwined. One widely circulated definition of e-government formulated by several countries is as follows: "…the continuous innovation in the delivery of services, citizen participation, and governance through the transformation of external and internal relationships by the use of information technology, especially the Internet" (Roy 2006b: 253). This definition usefully underscores the relational fluidity of public sector governance in more online and networked societies where the public is both consumer and citizen.

Tapscott and Williams (2006) push this relational fluidity much further by demonstrating the transformational power of 'mass collaboration'. Their central notion of wikieconomics—a basis for a new socio-economic paradigm driven by openness, information-sharing, and new forms of collective action due to collapsing communication and transaction costs, and accelerating innovation—is one that leverages the potential of a world personified by Web 2.0 and a digital infrastructure, not only for passively receiving information but also creating and sharing content in new ways. They demonstrate the manner by which the organizational forms and strategies emerging today bear little resemblance to the traditional corporate model that dominated much of the preceding century.

Although there is little reason to doubt that mass collaboration will indeed change most everything for organizations, precisely when and how it will do so invariably gives rise to tensions between incremental change on the one hand and more holistic innovation on the other hand. Such tensions between tradition and transformation are particularly prevalent in the public sector where larger organizations and wider accountabilities to all citizens often create greater aversion to risk, especially on a systemic scale. Despite the tremendous changes ushered in during the past fifteen years, changes to public sector organizing principles and democratic institutions have been, on the whole, more evolutionary than revolutionary. In the absence of an acute crisis, government service transformation efforts must therefore balance the stability of incremental performance improvements on the one hand, with the need to innovative more radically on the other hand. This latter need is most visibly associated with the emergence of a digital society and Internet-savvy citizens and—notwithstanding digital and demographic divides—it will only intensify in the future (much as pressures and opportunities are already apparent).

This chapter is premised on two assumptions: first, a better conceptual understanding of the potential of mass collaboration for public sector innovation in the realm of service delivery is a useful undertaking; and second, any such potential must be examined within the contours of current models of service delivery and public sector management. Accordingly, this chapter aims to examine the nexus between public sector service transformation and the emerging phenomena of mass collaboration and to:

- elucidate emerging trends associated with Web 2.0 and the implications for public sector service delivery;
- examine how mass collaboration can contribute to collective learning and participative service design; and
- look ahead to prospects for transforming public sector governance with regards to public service design and delivery.

In addition, due to an increasingly digital and networked environment, both personified and shaped by mass collaboration, it is essential to consider how different levels of government can sort out their respective roles and identify opportunities for collaboration in order to create public value. A world driven by Web 2.0 suggests a set of organizational models and customer-citizen centric objectives—coupled with changing social expectations and values—that may not easily align with traditional jurisdictional boundaries both within and across levels of government. For instance, the term 'federated architecture' for better information sharing and service integration implies a level of seamless coordination that is far removed from traditional forms of political federalism that emphasize sovereignty and separate domains (and by extension silos).

This chapter will first examine the rise of Web 2.0, wikieconomics and more collaborative and networked service ecosystems, as well as the tensions between such trends and traditional principles of public sector organization. Accordingly, it is also necessary to consider the fluidity of sectoral boundaries (i.e., public, private, non-profit) due to heightened pressures for collaboration between industry and government; greater potential for information sharing; and new mixes of delivery channels. Then it probes the importance of knowledge management and shared learning capacities for collective intelligence to service innovation in a more digitally and socially networked environment. Lastly it assesses how governments have fared to date in transcending organizational and jurisdictional boundaries.

Web 2.0 and service ecosystems

Web 2.0 has emerged as a proxy not only for new technological capacities but also for a new social paradigm with sweeping implications for organizations in all sectors. The *Wikipedia* definition of Web 2.0 is as follows: "Web 2.0 is a term describing the trend in the use of World Wide Web technology and Web design that aims to enhance creativity, information sharing, and, most notably, collaboration among users".[1] This latter emphasis on collaboration is the linchpin between Web 2.0 as an evolving, more interactive and participative online architecture on the one hand, and the notion of 'wikinomics' introduced by Tapscott and Williams (2006) on the other hand.

The essence of wikinomics is a wave of 'mass collaboration that changes everything' via dramatically reduced transaction costs and revolutionary opportunities for mobilizing knowledge, skills and resources in new ways. As Williams puts it:

> Already, millions of people have joined forces in self-organized collaborations that have produced dynamic innovations in goods and services rivaling the world's largest and best-financed enterprise networks. If masses of ordinary people can peer-produce an operating system (Linux), an encyclopedia (Wikipedia), the media (YouTube/Current TV), a mutual fund, and even a physical thing such as a motorcycle, one should carefully consider what might come next (Williams 2008).

Williams adds that "the emerging 'age of participation' presents an historic occasion to fundamentally redesign how government operates, how and what the public sector provides, and ultimately, how governments interact and engage with their citizens" (Ibid.). In helping to frame prospects for positive innovation, it is possible to articulate some key differences between what might be termed Government 1.0 (the traditional paradigm of public sector management and accountability) and Government 2.0 (what lies ahead in an era of mass collaboration). Differences between the two perspectives on public sector organizing principles and conduct have been well illustrated by figure 1 developed by Deloitte Research.

Figure 1: Government 1.0 versus 2.0

Dimension	Government 1.0	Government 2.0
Operating model	• Hierarchical • Rigid	• Networked • Collaborative • Flexible
New models of service delivery	• One-size-fits-all • Monopoloy • Single channel	• Personalized • Choice-based • Multi-channel
Performance-driven	• Input-oriented • Closed	• Outcome-driven • Transparent
Decision-making	• Spectator	• Participative

Source: Deloitte Research, 2008. Available at: www.deloitte.com/assets/Dcom-Canada/Local%20Assets/Documents/ca_govt_web20_mar08_EN.pdf.

The 2007 Accenture global survey on e-government and service transformation portrays this sort of evolution (or shift to the right as seen in figure 1) as less a choice than necessity in today's networked era. Indeed, what emerges from this review and others such as the United Nations 2008 Global e-Government Survey is a clear indication that governments around the world are actively subscribing to Government 2.0 principles—even as the results to date in terms of service improvement are mixed. One challenge in particular is to adapt both structurally and culturally to the fluidity and complexity of today's organizational and technological environment and the imperative of interdependent linkages and shared capacities which results:

> As governments look to the future they realize they cannot deliver on the full promise of leadership in customer service on their own. Their linear,

process-oriented business models are evolving into complex ecosystems of citizens, communities, business partners, non-governmental organizations, and other stakeholders, all of which take on a share of responsibility for developing and providing value-led services (Accenture 2007: 8).

The notion of an 'ecosystem' has become an increasingly prominent lens in recent years through which to understand new patterns of both governance and management (Paquet 1997; Hamel and Breen 2007). Within the language of industry and the marketplace, the main premise underpinning the concept of an ecosystem is a shift from independence (i.e., a single firm) toward interdependence and a variety of collaborative relationships that are increasingly central and strategic to the performance of a corporate enterprise that, in turn, must become less hierarchical and insular and more open and adaptable (Ibid.). Although this trend predates the mainstream expansion of the Internet during the past decade, it follows that online connectivity and the expansion of virtual forms of communicating and organizing greatly facilitate the rise of interdependence.

As Tapscott and Williams explain, central to the emergence of this new paradigm is "the declining cost of collaborating" (Tapscott and Williams 2006: 55):

All of this leads to what we and our colleagues call 'Coase's law': A firm will tend to expand until the costs of organizing an extra transaction within the firm become equal to the cost of carrying out the same transaction on the open market...How has the Internet affected Coase's law? Strictly speaking, the law remains as valid as ever. But the Internet has caused transaction costs to plunge so steeply that it has now become more useful to read Coase's law, in effect, backward: Normally firms should shrink until the costs of performing a transaction internally no longer exceeds the cost of performing it externally (Ibid., 56).

This fundamental shift in cost dynamics—coupled with what the same authors term as 'platforms for participation' and the 'wiki workplace'—fuel a collaborative ethos that characterizes the more open, shared and technological infrastructure that Web 2.0 provides. In a complementary examination of mass collaboration's poster child, *Wikipedia*, Shirky dissects an 'unmanaged division of labour' that underpins a new organizational model that transcends the choice between market and firm. The key to success is that "because contributors aren't employees, a wiki can take a staggering amount of input with a minimum of overhead" (Shirky 2008: 120). Furthermore, the author explains how the open-source-inspired model of content provision and constant peer review fuel constant adaptation and quality control in a manner that the traditional forms of corporate specialization and supervision can simply not generate (Ibid.).

A key insight provided by Shirky is his formulation of a wiki as a 'hybrid of tool and community' and the power of the latter in generating commitment and engagement amongst members who not only choose to partake in this creative process but also nurture an attachment to its principles and outputs.

This point is central to the prospective emergence of a Government 2.0 order since the traditional approach to governing has been to equate democratic legitimacy with the power of coercion (a power reinforced within the public service via a vertical chain of command and limited information flows), while most recent e-government models emphasize a competitive order premised upon customer service and choice, and improved efficiency. What's missing in this realm of government reform today is a new basis for collaboration and engagement at many levels: a new employee compact for public servants; a new organizational architecture for departments and agencies; and ultimately a new form of social contract for democracy itself.

New sectoral mixes
Understanding government's uniqueness is an important precursor to prescribing reform. While the trend in recent times has been a *de facto* benchmarking of industry and government performance suggesting a convergence of experiences and approaches, as Blakemore points out the "obligations of being a customer are not easily linked with the complexities of being a citizen. However, Public Value may involve similar bilateral obligations such as those emerging in business" (Blakemore 2006: 1).

The author, therefore, calls for a cautious approach in learning from but not necessarily seeking to emulate the experiences from industry. The emergence of 'public value', a theme returned to more fully in the next section, points to the importance of finding new hybrid models of public and private interests and corresponding governance models to underpin them (Kettl 2005; Stoker 2006). Indeed, *Wikipedia*'s non-profit status provides a prospective third ownership and governance realm to this co-evolutionary mix (Shirky 2008). The central point here is that with respect to new service delivery models, stark traditional choices between public and private ownership are less likely to prevail than blurred sector boundaries and collaborative structures that open up new forms of engagement and accountability.

In addition to ownership and control, this inter-mixing of sectoral activity is also essential to navigating the increasingly abundant and networked information flows that are the lifeblood of Web 2.0 and the mass collaboration movement. Blakemore points out that "the cross-matching of citizen data, with commercial data can generate new insights into service demands and delivery" (Blakemore 2006: 4). This point closely aligns with the notion of re-intermediation, as any number of information sources and processes from different sectors can be gathered (potentially by service providers or service users) and repackaged into bundled and integrated service offerings that offer more value for the user.

Many important challenges must be addressed, notably concerns about privacy and if and how information is shared. While some commentators in Anglo-Saxon democracies are often tempted to lament service integration efforts (and related information processes tied to surveillance for example) as trampling privacy rights, it bears noting that the leading e-government jurisdictions of the world in Scandinavia are seemingly able to marry technological prowess and interoperability across sectors on the one hand, and high levels of transparency and trust on the other hand. Accordingly, Scandinavian countries (clustered at the top of the 2008 UN global e-government survey) have led the world in developing pre-filled tax returns sent out to citizens for verification and acceptance (or correction if need be), an initiative dependent upon more widely accepted information sharing practices across the public and private sectors. In Canada, by contrast, the primary thrust of public sector service transformation, in terms of the role of the private sector, has been in partnering to upgrade the internal channels and capacities of government (and as such industry is an externalized partner contributing to this process). The emergence of Web 2.0 and the notion of service ecosystems call into question this logic in asking whether or not it makes sense for government to exclusively deliver specific services. As Gartner points out:

> Web 2.0 will seriously challenge the tenets of current e-government strategies, leading to a revision of the whole approach to citizen centricity and moving the 'one-stop-shop' away from being a government portal. As a consequence, citizen online behaviour will be less predictable (Gartner 2007: 1).

This quote reveals what is likely to be a critical shift in terms of public sector service delivery capacities in an era of Web 2.0 and mass collaboration, namely the inability of governments to predict user behaviour and strategize in a rational and linear way as to service offerings and 'channel' usage. This is not to say that governments can no longer plan, but rather that the nature of such service design processes and the ensuing formulation of business models to underpin them is likely to become a good deal more dynamic. Thus there will be a much greater dependence upon adaptive capacities within the public sector tied to partnerships and networks involving a variety of external stakeholders. Accordingly, one of the most important unknowns in this regard is the extent to which a multi-channel delivery strategy can and should encompass the usage of delivery channels owned and maintained by private and non-profit delivery actors.

As articulated by a recent report of the Government of New Zealand, a more strategic nexus between planning, communication and engagement presents itself:

> ...Strategic planning for Web 2.0 initiatives is expected to become increasingly important in the future...As agencies begin to participate in third-party sites, or consider setting up places in virtual worlds (such as Second Life), they may need to establish virtual government strategies that define how they will engage in a variety of virtual communities, ranging from internal communities to external communities where they reach out to the public (New Zealand 2007, chapter 6).

As government moves from electronic service delivery to administering 'mashable' Web services, non-government organizations might mix government information with content from other sources on their own Web applications. Agencies will need to consider the boundaries of their responsibility and accountability for information they provide. Furthermore, increasingly, agencies might present information sourced from outside government on their own websites; this will raise questions about the extent to which government is responsible for the quality of that information, and whether it is important for the user to be able to differentiate between government and non-government sources of information (Ibid.).

Evolving service ecosystems comprising public, private and non-profit actors call into question the notion that any one government can unilaterally and effectively manage its own multi-channel framework while ensuring constant adaptation. A particular challenge here for government lies in the creation and addition of new delivery channels, such as mobile phones.

As wireless phone penetration rises, the usage of mobile delivery channels can be expected to follow suit along with key strategic choices for government in terms of maintaining multiple delivery channels, as well as providing incentives for service users to shift from traditional forms of infrastructure (such as paper and in-person centres) to more virtual forms of interaction. In 2007, for example, Singapore displaced Canada as the highest ranked country in Accenture's global survey of e-government and customer-centric strategies—an achievement, built to a significant degree, upon the expansion of mobile delivery channels:

> While Singapore exhibits strength in multichannel integration, its clear intent is to continue to push its tech-savvy citizens toward efficient online channels, particularly mobile channels. Singapore has one of the world's highest mobile penetration rates; currently citizens and businesses have mobile access to approximately 150 government services, with mGovernment becoming an increasingly important delivery channel. The government aims to have at least 300 mGovernment services available by 2008. In addition, in July of 2006, the government also introduced a common SMS number 74688 (SGOVT) and format for new SMS-based government mobile services, to simplify use for customers. Future service channel options may include voice recognition and interactive TV— both of which the government has recently piloted (Accenture 2007: 113).

This accelerating pace of technological innovation in terms of channel options—akin to something of a technological treadmill for government service providers—augments the importance of coordination and collective learning between all sectors. Beyond sectoral collaboration, mass collaboration also affords a much greater opportunity for service users to directly engage in contributing to the collective intelligence of a given jurisdiction.

Knowledge management, collective intelligence and service design

This '2.0' emphasis on collaboration and openness is closely intertwined with the concept of 'collective intelligence' as a basis for shared learning and the potential for mass collaboration to foster innovation and better decision-making capacities (Coe, Paquet and Roy 2001; Griffiths 2001; Allen et al. 2005). Such capacities matter in an environment that may well shift away from 'single-window' solutions to multiple ecosystems and delivery means. Tapscott, Williams and Herman articulate the manner by which the pursuit of service improvement and public value is increasingly a collaborative affair pursued via mass collaboration and 'governance webs':

> These networks of public, private and/or civil society participants will deliver government services or enable stakeholder participation in government processes. After all, in a complex and interdependent world no individual – and certainly no company or government – is an island. To succeed, governments must learn how to collaborate more effectively with other governments and a diverse array of social organizations (Tapscott, Williams and Herman 2008: 4).

One conceptual lens for such widened participation and learning is the presentation of 'public value management' as a 'new narrative for networked governance' (Stoker 2006). Explicitly contrasted with hierarchical and control-minded public sector traditions, as well as the competitive and customer-focused business mentality of new public management (NPM), public value management (PVM) is premised on partnership, nuance and dialogue:

> The key point in understanding public value management...starts with the understanding that preferences are not formed in a vacuum and should not be taken as given. Part of the challenge of public managers is to engage in a dialogue with the public about their preferences but in a way that allows for deliberation about choices and alternatives...Discovering preferences involves a complex dialogue so that efficiency and accountability are trading partners, not the objects of a trade-off (Ibid., 51).

Therefore it may be possible for the public to act as either customer or citizen, depending on the circumstance and need—and more importantly—the legitimacy of both roles must be built into governance. Stoker argues that PVM is the only sort of governance paradigm that can adequately address the complexity and interdependencies of today's governance and managerial systems, which demand a renewed reconciliation of the often conflicting demands of efficiency, accountability and equity. PVM embraces a much more multi-faceted set of relationships, both within the public sector and between governments and other stakeholders including the public.[2] In doing so, PVM requires a robust and shared knowledge management infrastructure enjoining governments, all sectors and the broader public at large.

This knowledge management infrastructure will be increasingly intertwined with the information flows and active participation of stakeholders and individuals that comprise Web 2.0's facilitation of 'new governance webs for service delivery.' Tapscott, Williams and Herman point to four central issues confronting public sector service providers:

- The opportunity to exploit Web 2.0 technologies to deliver responsive, high quality, consistent, end-to-end service tailored to the unique needs of individual constituents and customer segments;
- The increasing need for time-and-resource-constrained agencies to take advantage of external knowledge and expertise through new models of 'crowdsourcing';
- The challenges of managing private sector participation in service delivery webs as corporations weigh up opportunities to enter public markets; and
- The opportunity to turn formerly passive recipients of public services into active 'prosumers' who play an important and ongoing role in creating public value (Tapscott, Williams and Herman 2008: 10).

The second and forth points in particular underscore the new knowledge management template that is less (though still) about information flows within individual organizations and more about capturing information from a multitude of sources and transforming that information into shared learning and actionable innovation.

In 2006, the Scottish government undertook a major service transformation exercise predicated on consultation and dialogue with key stakeholders involved in service delivery both inside and outside of the public service including the citizenry. With regards to consulting the public, the purpose has been less about gauging satisfaction levels with existing service processes and more about engaging citizens in a conversation about the evolution of public service delivery. Priorities and concerns and key design principles were sought. Key messages from public service users included wanting to:

- be treated as a person;[3]
- know how and where to complain about problems in public services;
- be involved in designing and deciding about the services in their area;
- hold public services to account on the things that matter to them;
- be told when important changes are made to public services; and
- have access to skilled front-line workers (Scottish Executive 2006).

The last point raises some important questions pertaining to the multi-channel strategy of the public sector, including not only the relative mix of channels (and incentives for using them), but also the degree of tangible presence by government in a given community. Here the inclusion of the third point—the involvement of the user in the deciding and designing of service—suggests a participatory link between service, policy and community learning and growth.

Although this link may appear rather innocuous at first glance, it denotes a significant change in tone with respect to how the Scottish government and the citizenry discuss service. The significance stems from a willingness by the government to acknowledge a need to step beyond the usual service transformation rhetoric that characterizes the public as largely interested only in outcomes and the sorts of measures of customer service akin to marketplace experiences.

Consistent with the notions above of a service ecosystem and public value management, a learning-based strategy of service delivery implies the gathering of information and the processing of such information into knowledge in order to constantly improve the efficiency and quality of service offerings. An ecosystem is thus akin to a smart community, both within and outside of the public sector, where the collective intelligence of all stakeholders—including service users—drives service innovation and performance improvement. It is the boundaries of this smart community that are increasingly fluid for the aforementioned reasons.

Whereas in the past senior officials from central agencies and specialized service providers (often in concert with outside specialists) have typically provided direction and prioritizing, participative service design in a Web 2.0 environment implies a more open and collaborative model of decision making that encompasses the input of a much wider network.

As the Government of New Zealand once again notes the governance consequences are profound:

Government services are expected increasingly to be accessed from channels outside government (such as banks, insurance companies, retailers, search engines, utilities, mobile operators, and social networks). Service delivery will require cooperation between different government agencies and other parties with responsibility for various elements of the process. This will lead to interesting governance challenges, requiring frameworks to be developed for managing these relationships. Furthermore, a new generation of governance processes and tools will be required to manage the evolution of electronic services that are cooperatively designed by constituents, as well as information (such as wikis) that can be modified by hundreds or thousands of different people (New Zealand 2007: chapter 6).

This new generation of governance processes extends far beyond the still important but insufficient focus on internal infrastructure for information sharing and interoperability (typically called the service-oriented architecture). While gathering and sharing information across government is important (for joined-up services for example), insights must also be gathered from a myriad of sources including (potentially) front-line delivery staff, policy departments, service users themselves, and a variety of service intermediaries—all potentially enjoined through new learning networks. It is this latter dynamic that is the basis of shared knowledge and learning.

There is a resulting need to reframe the traditional perspective of knowledge management as a mainly internal set of tools and processes to one more broadened and consistent with notions of mass-collaboration, service ecosystems and Web 2.0. In particular, knowledge generation must be viewed as a set of shared and collective processes enjoining participants both within and outside of the service provider. As one commentary put it:

Web 2.0 platforms are changing our concept of knowledge management by shifting the knowledge frontier outwards. As knowledge becomes more external to our organisations, perhaps even created by customers themselves, success is increasingly dependent on how internal and external information is combined, analysed and acted upon (Guan 2008: April 8).

The design and deployment of such broadened knowledge management systems presents important challenges for government in terms of its own internal capacities as well as collaborative capacities with technical experts (i.e., knowledge management vendors) and the broader community of potential users and partners. Knowledge management efforts within government have typically fallen short due to an overly technical focus—a focus on apparatus as opposed to people and processes and how such knowledge is ultimately used (Kettl 2005). Governments should be thinking about what sorts of tools and technologies are most likely to augment the shared learning capacities of their extended service ecosystems, from within which participative service design capacities for innovation and constant improvement are likely to emerge.

Indeed, here is where there is an important alignment between how mainly internal information architectures are designed and this extended view of knowledge management. The alignment stems from the growing potential for value added from open standards and open source systems that reduce the transaction costs of working collaboratively.

Transcending boundaries

The internal transformation efforts of many governments have both confronted and created considerable tensions between department and agency-specific strategies on the one hand and cross-governmental integrated service capacities on the other hand. These latter initiatives (e.g., integrated portals based upon life events and client streams; one-stop call centres; no-wrong-door models of customer service; etc.) require service and enterprise architectures that facilitate interoperability, collaborative action and, ultimately, shared accountability (Langford and Roy 2008b). Many such initiatives have been partially or fully stymied by a range of now well-documented barriers to such integrative action, most of them embedded in the vertical, silo-based mentality and managerial structures traditionally found in government (Roy 2006 a, b).

A particular challenge is whether integrative action should be ordained in a top-down manner—often led by those forces and actors orchestrating the centralizing tendencies—or instead nurtured in a more organic, bottom-up manner where departments and agencies are supported with information and incentives to join us as they see fit, ideally upon identification of mutually beneficial opportunities. In trying to achieve an optimal balance, New Zealand is an interesting case study in this regard. A traditionally decentralized public sector with more passively supportive central agencies encouraging rather than directing departments and agencies, efforts have gradually been cultivated to nurture more integrated cross-governmental infrastructure and initiatives:

> In 2004, agencies were, almost without exception, using information and communication technologies (ICT) to improve staff access to information. Once services for New Zealanders were primarily based around individual agencies, requiring customers to contact several agencies to complete related transactions and processes. By 2005, the number of channels and services available online were increasing and agencies were starting to integrate their services, grouping them to allow New Zealanders single-point access to services originating from different agencies. Successful integration of technological systems underpinning the cross-agency service had resulted in measurable efficiency improvements. More importantly, it signified the increasing integration of processes among agencies at not only the technological but also the business and relationship level. In 2007, the beginnings of a trend are apparent, towards working more collaboratively with the support of major all-of-government infrastructure. The Government Logon Service (GLS) and Government Shared Network (GSN), intended to serve as platforms to cross-agency services in the future, have been built and their operations are gaining momentum. There are notable examples of system infrastructure being built on the basis of cross-sector collaborations – a change which is driven by both technological factors and business needs. Sectoral ICT strategies are reinforcing a whole-of-sector view in planning to strengthen the operational and management infrastructure of agencies to serve sector interests (New Zealand 2007: 111).

A critically important question for the future of public sector service transformation is whether or not such a vision is desirable and consistent with an environment characterized by mass collaboration, Web 2.0 and service ecosystems. The risk is that if such seamless governance arrangements are sought in an overly centralized manner (formulated in similarly linear models of planning and resourcing), systemic innovation for citizen-centric solutions will be constrained. In other words, misinterpreted, such a portrait of seamlessness can easily translate into a single provider (department or agency) consolidating service offerings and channels within its midst. If unaccompanied by a culture that supports genuinely collaborative arrangements across different units of government, such a single provider can easily be perceived as a threat rather than a potential partner.

While some proponents of a more centralized architecture may have benefited in the early days of e-government and electronic service delivery—due to the novelty of such developments and a focus on automation that more or less standardized service users as customers seeking efficiency and choice—the complementary logics of collective intelligence and public value management suggest an alternative, far less linear path. Instead of a single service architecture for a government as a whole, multiple service ecosystems may be expected to form (and ideally should be encouraged to do so), the parameters of which are formulated not by government planners but by, at least in part, virtual networks of citizens and stakeholders engaged in a constant dialogue on how best to do so.

A key challenge for the public sector thus lies in balancing three simultaneous sets of forces: i) in presenting a more integrated front-end face to the user (who may well be seeking simplicity and one point of access); ii) reconfiguring the back-office functions of government in a manner that supports integrative services where warranted (i.e., demanded and deemed beneficial to both users and government); and iii) facilitating knowledge sharing and learning (i.e., collective intelligence) across the public sector in a manner that encourages innovation and collaborative networks where there are reasons and incentives to do so. This challenge, considerable as it is for single government—especially at the national level—becomes wider and more complex when accounting for a jurisdiction as a whole and multiple government levels.

Conclusion – Will Web 2.0 change everything?

One of the most significant challenges facing the public sector today in terms of Web 2.0 adoption and service delivery innovation is the widening segmentation—mainly, though not exclusively, along demographic lines—between those service users and recipients that are now routinely online (not only passively searching information but more actively engaging in participative mechanisms of one sort or another) and those that continue to be reticent in doing so.

Before Web 2.0, within the realm of e-government and online service, learning was relatively static—limited to user surveys of one sort or another (such as the example of Canada's much famed Citizens First surveys). With Web 2.0 emerging as a driver of more interactive and dynamic learning and consistent with a culture of mass collaboration (individually and organizationally), a much more collective engagement process is required consistent with the adoption of collective intelligence across an entire service ecosystem.

The starting point, then, for a government's service transformation strategy in the emerging era of Web 2.0 and mass collaboration is to facilitate the widest possible set of dialogues—as it is naive to presume that government can establish and maintain a single venue that can prove sufficient—across service users, providers and partners.

Early public opinion data suggests that governments enjoy a level of support from the public to pursue the transformational potential of Web 2.0 for service and democratic renewal.[4] Yet polls and surveys cannot be enough to gather the tacit knowledge of those citizens (or customers in the service realm) proving to be early adapters to new social networking platforms, mobile channels and the like.

It is important to underscore how the urgency for governments may at times be both understated and overstated. In terms of the former, clearly any level of service satisfaction at present cannot be viewed today as reason for inaction given the widening expansion of online communities and virtual channels. With regards to the latter, however, active Web 2.0 usage remains limited to a relatively small segment of the population, presenting an opportunity for public sector providers to not radically re-organize themselves to the whims of this early-adopter group but instead to engage them as an important source of learning and knowledge. And it is here, once again, where demographics becomes so crucial since the dilemma for government is a relatively aging cadre of senior managers far removed from the realities of newer generations of workers growing up in an Internet and, more recently, a Web 2.0 era. One recent survey of two thousand undergraduate students in Canada,[5] for example, found that some ninety percent of this group regularly used social networking tools, a trend with unquestionable ripple effects in the workplace in all sectors—as Tapscott and Williams illustrate in their own formulation of *Wikinomics*.

Striking the necessary balance in going forward requires a Web 2.0 strategy that is more bottom-up than top-down, particularly in building bridges between senior managers (and elected officials) currently in place and new and prospective employees with alternative perceptions and new insights to share. One provincial crown corporation in Canada, for instance, struck a dialogue between senior executives and university students in order to undertake a website redesign and broader customer engagement strategy. These sorts of micro-level initiatives—encouraged across a multitude of departments and agencies and jurisdictions—are more likely to yield systemic change than grandiose schemes and master plans that lack the capacities with which to follow through. The Government of Canada's recent decision to largely abandon its secure channel apparatus—for online identity authentication and transactions—is a vivid illustration of the perils of excessive control, both within government and in terms of working in concert with the private sector.[6]

With regards to looking ahead, Web 2.0 and collaborative innovations emerging through experimental processes are all the more likely to be poorly suited to central coordination. For many governments, embracing this sort of organic approach to mass collaboration and Web 2.0 innovation may not fit easily with the emphasis during the past decade on integrated portals and specialized service providers. Yet it may well be time to rethink the function of such service entities—as less about integration across government (and less still about fully integrated systems across governments) and more about facilitation and learning. While there is likely to be some public value in a single-window interface between a government and its citizenry providing information and direction to those in need, many 'customers' of government will be seeking more tailored bundles of services across a multitude of wired and wireless channels that are unlikely to be full under the purview of the public sector.

Service entities can thus be important stakeholders in providing overall guidance to public sector bodies and in helping to identify opportunities for partnership (both within and across jurisdictions and sectors), but they should not be imposing strategy and objectives. Their role is somewhat akin to many CIO functions that have sought to balance interoperability across government with more individualized units and clusters of units responsible for the final adaptation and alignment of technology, policy and performance. For some jurisdictions, embracing flexibility and pursuing such a collaborative mindset is self-evident; elsewhere it may represent a more significant departure from traditional practice as stakeholders in the executive branch (both political and administrative) seek to preserve their authority in a manner consistent with Government 1.0 and much of e-government's early stages.

Government 2.0 is about rethinking power in the pursuit of integrative outcomes—harnessing the potential of mass collaboration—and the changes required are multi-faceted and as much institutional and cultural as technological. Not everything will change, but in ten years time it is a good bet that the service delivery apparatus of the public sector will be a good deal more diffuse than at present (across both sectoral and jurisdictional boundaries) and a good deal more participatory in terms of user involvement and co-evolutionary service design.

Endnotes

1 http://en.wikipedia.org/wiki/Web_2

2 This view is notably consistent with a recent and thoughtful consideration of the impacts of online connectivity and digital technology and democracy—and the importance of reconfiguring government-public engagements, enhancing the communicative power of citizens, and refurbishing legislative bodies and processes accordingly (Dutton and Peitu 2007).

3 This point may carry important repercussions for channel management in a more public-centric world. For example, polling conducted by Service Canada in 2006 found that people preferred the characterization of 'citizen' over that of 'customer' in dealing with public sector providers. The tendency is to view citizen or client-based relationships as more dependent on a human interface than on virtual channels. Nonetheless, this view also requires nuance as demonstrated by the case of Denmark where governments are attempting to balance mandatory electronic channels nationally with a front-line human interface municipally.

4 The Government of Canada commissioned polling on public attitudes toward Web 2.0, the results of which were presented at June 2008 Lac Carling meetings as well as at the GTEC professional development and trade show in October 2008.

5 The study, reported on by IT World Canada, was conducted by Professor Avner Levin at Ryerson University's School of Business Management.

6 See Kathryn May's piece in the *Ottawa Citizen* on October 18, 2008: "Government to replace $1B online service boondoggle".

CONCLUSION

Now the Real Work Begins...

As this book neared completion, the Canada Revenue Agency (CRA) aired television ads that evocatively illustrated both the promise and realities of the 'service state'. The commercial aimed to inform citizens on how they could take advantage of tax credits—admittedly a visual challenge to any advertisement producer. The image presented was of women and men literally pulling words from above their heads as they walked down some aimless path. They accumulated them in their arms as the voice-over informed the viewer that the Government of Canada made numerous tax credits available. The message was also that it was up to the citizen to keep informed of the hundreds of possibilities.

It was a visually pleasant advertisement that offered an attractive message: citizens were offered a chance to reduce the taxes they owe to the Canadian government. As such, it presented a good example of effective delivery of a key message.

The CRA undoubtedly reached hundreds of thousands with this imaginative commercial. By making sure the tax credits were explained on its website, it was fulfilling its mission of making information available. And certainly, by allowing Canadians to file their taxes online (and citizens—or rather their tax preparers—have been record-setting, early adopters of this method), CRA has improved its services. It continually receives good grades for customer care and has done impressive work in improving the quality of its services. According to the Citizens First surveys, its staff is rated as knowledgeable, fair, efficient and courteous—not an easy feat in the tax collecting business. Notwithstanding its successes, CRA is also emblematic of what is wrong about the service state.

The CRA certainly did not reach all taxpayers, and it is doubtful that Canadians will fully claim the tax credits they deserve because they will have been unaware or been confused about what exactly a tax credit really is. The 'service state' was supposed to bring about a new understanding of service—of finding new ways to reach citizens, of pushing more comprehensive solutions to those looking for them. It was supposed to be about creating new services in a cost-effective manner that could bring in more revenue. It was also about being more responsive to a wider range of citizens in need of services. This vision has not come through and we fear that the state is on the wrong path. Instead of new discoveries, new services and new approaches, the state is merely providing the same services—but faster, cheaper and, in some cases, around the clock. The service state has not lived up to its mission. Instead it has created a self-serve state where citizens are presented with a salad bar of goods and an invitation to help themselves. We are mindful of the fact that many public sector organizations have done stellar work in crafting creative partnerships with private sector companies, non-profit agencies, and each other in providing excellent service, but a whiff of complacency has set in and too many are tempted to sit on their laurels and indulge in self-congratulation.

What has gone wrong? We asked six basic questions and found that the service state has avoided finding the answers to critical problems. Instead of seeking to transform services by expanding and integrating them, it has contented itself with muddling through issues, perhaps in the hope that solutions will eventually present themselves. There was urgency to our enquiry. Public services have had a tremendous window of opportunity to experiment with new methods, new understandings and new technologies but have come up wanting. Why is that?

Our first question was to ask who the service state is really serving: *customers, clients,* or *citizens?* The answer, of course, is that the state serves all, but what is striking is that the real progress in service delivery has been made in serving customers. In turn, this has dominated the thinking of the state, and, we fear, steered it in the wrong direction. This can be explained for a number of reasons.

First, it was a relatively easy thing to do. *Customers* are the citizens that are either required to have contact with the state or simply choose to. In that sense, a customer is someone who needs to get a driver's licence, or renew one. It can also be a person who wishes, in most provinces, to buy alcohol. In that case, say, a citizen living in Ontario who wishes to purchase a fine bottle of wine will go to the most convenient outlet of the Liquor

Control Board of Ontario (LCBO) and will enter a clean, well-lit, well-situated store that will boast a wide range of products. Most customers of the LCBO emerge from the experience quite happy—the service state has done its job. The same thing can be said about the driver's licence. It is a product the state 'sells' in a manner that it uses for all its citizens—an automated, uncomplicated, practically friction-free process. By investing in these services, it is not surprising that the service state has done well in serving customers.

What about *clients*? These are people who may not be so interested in getting state services, but need them. In this category are the citizens who need health care, social services, policing or income support. Their experiences are more complicated. Their needs are confused and unclear, and their hope is to have a more customized experience. The problem is that as the service state adopts a customer focus it loses its drive to serve the more expensive needs of the client. The service state should be investing more research into what the client needs, but instead has fallen under the spell of pursuing the almighty customer, resulting in a frustrating neglect.

And what about the *citizen*? The citizen either benefits or loses from all transactions—if the vulnerable client does not get the right service at the right time, more tax dollars may be lost as solutions to complicating problems become more expensive. For example, if illegal guns are allowed into the country, it is lives that will pay. Where does the citizen fit in this service state? In such cases, the citizens are served in two principal ways: by demonstrating, with as much transparency as possible, how the money was spent; and by seeking the input of the citizen in determining how services should be deployed. We have found that the state has not been innovative in seeking input from citizens—people who inevitably will become, at one point or another in their lives, both clients and customers of the service state.

Instead, the service state has focused its quality control efforts on occasional customers for some of the routine services of the state. We have found the strategy wanting. Rather than expanding the focus of enquiry onto a wider range of *clients* and *citizens*, the state has, through adoption of the Citizen First survey approach, been content to keep asking essentially the same questions of its *customers*, hoping to see some improvement in scores around indicators such as courtesy and accessibility.

The surveys cannot do much more than point to a certain level of satisfaction, but we contend that that is the wrong question asked of the wrong people. There should be more to the service state's enquiries than to ask if customers are happy with the basics of what they wanted. More egregious is the claim that customer satisfaction with routine services leads to a confidence in the state's legitimacy. Why not ask about other perceived needs or, indeed, work towards better understanding of unperceived needs? (Think of the tax credit issue). There are numerous examples of inexpensive methods available to seek input from the citizenry on services, and we are confident that public servants can apply them. What is needed is political leadership, but we will come back to that later.

The second reason is the distraction over the 'culture' issue. This is not to say that there should be no concern about how employees treat citizens, or how the state treats its employees. But it has to go beyond those concerns. Governments have to find ways to balance more discretion in the hands of front-line public servants while at the same time ensure fair and just service for all. The reality is that many, if not most, of the front-line employees are as satisfied as they are likely to be under the current regime. For this to change, the system is going to have to change. We are confident that their ethics and personal inclinations motivate them to do well by the people who require service. The issue, however, is much more complicated. Public servants may well improve the quality of their services but, beyond wearing a pleasant smile and working diligently, most of the decisions on the factors of good quality service—training, knowledge, technology, discretion, effective and responsive partnerships—belong in the corner offices, not the service counter.

We have found that 'satisfaction' is as poor a measure of employee culture as it is of customer feelings. A satisfied employee may or may not be a good employee. Respondents to the employee surveys are merely showing whether they are satisfied with the environment in which they work. Our study of the publicly available surveys indeed confirms that most public employees are quite satisfied with their working conditions. For some government departments, this score equals a rate of 'engagement', but this can be misleading. Satisfaction with a job does not equal a commitment, and the categories used by governments are so broad as to make distinctions between levels of satisfaction impossible. Some will argue that finer-grained studies at the office or 'counter' level (which are not publicly available) will help identify areas where service will be improved. We are sceptical. Our hunch is that these studies will only determine if local directors or managers are effective. The solution is, inevitably, to get the non-functioning supervisor rotated out of the position, which may solve a local problem of satisfaction but will leave unanswered the question of how to improve service.

The service state was born of a double revolution that originated in the private sector: the discovery that *customers* really can be a source of wealth if their loyalty is sought (the private sector has no *clients* and *citizens* to cater to—they are too expensive); and dramatic technological advances. The state was slow in responding to the evolving needs of its customers and clients but on technological issues was completely at sea. It needed to forge partnerships with both sectors, and the results of its efforts have been mixed at best.

There is a third reason—a reluctance to yield to the basic demands of partnering—that is, to share decision making. The Weberian structure of government in Canada has been enduring, with a decision-making apparatus that is much more comfortable working on a vertical axis rather than horizontally. The obsession with upward accountability to risk-averse politicians has made service transformation difficult. It has been a difficult learning lesson for Canada's public services, and a costly one, as experiments with technology purveyors proved costly and had to be abandoned. In part, it was the fault of private sector vendors who did not understand the rigours and strictures of public services, including the need to work inexpensively and with transparency. It was also the fault of the public services, who too often did not understand the potential of the technology, let alone how it actually worked. There have been successes on this front, but the resistance to changing the decision-making paradigm has frustrated the development of a service state that is willing to experiment with new rules, new accountabilities and a renewed creativity.

The inability to share governance with partnering service organizations has also hamstrung the transformation. Demands for accountabilities of service-oriented non-profit and community groups—those groups who keep a close ear to the ground and can articulate needs on behalf of those who cannot—have multiplied and contradicted each other, while the state actively reduces its contributions and makes more demands on standards and rules. Non-profit organizations have been frustrated by the proliferation of 'red tape' and overcomplicated accountabilities that have transformed their organizations from care-focused entities devoted to clients to entities engaged in mass-processing customers.

The frustrating experience of trying to work horizontally has replicated itself in trying to work across jurisdictional boundaries. Of course, there have been exceptions—areas of public policy where governments have been working together to offer a better service experience to Canadians, but they are few and far between. The service state's promise—based on a new appreciation that the 'citizen comes first' and in using new technologies—has not yielded much fruit.

How can these frustrations be explained? It is a mix of factors that have come together to slow the development of the service state.

The first factor is that legislators in Canada have practically been AWOL (absent without leave) on the file. Debates in legislative assemblies and in the House of Commons have not made room for the service state. Politicians have not been interested in discovering new partnerships, or in discussing how accountabilities could be improved and streamlined to make more room for service improvements. They have not called upon the governments to conduct more experiments and to effectively measure results. There are no legislative committees on services, and no public consultations on particular services. Politicians like to react to crises and have been unhelpful in bringing about service transformation. Again, we can point to exceptions, but they are precious few and far between. We know that their campaigns to win support among their colleagues mostly fall on deaf ears.

This may have been a blessing in disguise for public servants, but we persist in thinking that, as representatives of the citizens, elected representatives should have more than a casual interest in how the state offers its services and should lead the debate on how the future should be shaped. The service state is more than the concern of the technocracy and requires the organized input of legislators. The bureaucracy charged with delivering the services would ultimately see its hands strengthened by the consistent involvement of legislators who are genuinely interested in making government service better.

A second factor has been the context in which the service state was born. The same pressures brought about by a new clientele that wants a wide range of services have yielded demands that services be offered at modest cost. To make things more difficult, governments have been reluctant to invest heavily in transforming services. The first wave of reform was concerned with adopting basic technologies, followed by the first steps towards an Internet presence. The Y2K issue consumed most service-oriented dollars at the turn of the century, while service consolidations in integrated entities focused minds in the early years of the 21st century.

The story of technological investment was not generally a happy one, it is fair to say. There was misfiring and many false starts that cost governments dearly. The net effect was also to stall the thinking on how technologies could transform services, instead of simply trying to adapt services. Governments often chose big solutions to small problems, instead of identifying the ends towards which they aimed their efforts.

The paucity of vision documents around service improvements bears rich testimony to this reality.

A third factor has been public sector leadership. We salute the policy and operation entrepreneurs who have worked doggedly to convince colleagues in their departments, in other departments and in other governments that the service agenda was important. If Canada is—notwithstanding our critique—often a winner in various international contests, it is entirely the result of capable, public-spirited champions of continuously improving public service. The sad reality is that they have often been voices crying in the desert—and too often their demands for a heightened awareness of service needs have been met with shrugs and inertia.

The reality is that the leadership has been largely born from the public service, with very little successful integration of private sector executives with deep experience in service operations. For a generation now, 'service thinking' has been done by public sector executives with little or no experience in developing new services. The result has been that government services innovated in their delivery, but not in their nature. Service delivery lost an opportunity to begin reinvention; instead, it was mired in layers of accepted practices, bureaucratic constraints, outdated accountability demands and technological habits of the past.

This has impaired the creation an effective policy feedback loop. The service state has, so far, focused its attention on providing better access, leaving aside the more important task of integrating what is being learned about service back into the policy cycle. The ability to transform data into knowledge about the strengths, weaknesses and, indeed, relevance of programs and policies has not been evident. However, the adoption of new technologies, of creative partnerships and of a closer relationship with customers was supposed to facilitate this activity. There are signs of change such as the adoption of 311 systems in various cities, but the reality is that governments have moved terribly slowly in this direction. There is little evidence that service improvements so far have had any success in changing policy substantively.

There is great promise that government services can take a giant leap forward. Web 2.0 technology opens a new window for dramatic service innovation, but for the service state to really live up to its promise a new approach must be sought. For one thing, the citizen—not just the customer—must be probed about needs, both met and unmet. The new technologies will make it easier to ask the citizen about unrecognized needs, but it will be up to the state to convert the data it collects into a workable knowledge-driven agenda. There may be an opportunity for experimentation and for development of new services, both independently and in partnership with the business and the non-profit sector.

There is urgency to our plea. In the age when the private sector's energy and creativity can easily duplicate state activity (think of Google's area-mapping or the many companies now planning space flights), the public space is being threatened. The private sector's genius has been geared to finding solutions for new customers—and has done extremely well in this regard. The public sphere may want to yield its more mundane, routine activities but it must, like the private sector, develop value-added products that will respond to unmet needs where *citizens*, as *clients*, will be willing to pay extra for better or more comprehensive service.

This is not an easy territory to map out, but if the public sector does not do it, it will be done by the private sector. In that situation, the relevance of the public sector will be lost, and perhaps be limited to commissioning the important work to others.

The service state must ask new questions to achieve its vision. These are what we think are the most critical ones:

Are we measuring what matters? Good administrative practice requires an ongoing quality check on services. We note that progress has been made in many jurisdictions on this front, but there is a need to improve the system of monitoring quality, and this should be transparent. It is important, but not enough, to know if a service was delivered as promised. The service state must also ask if the right service was delivered to the right people at the right time.

Are we learning yet? Government departments should undertake rigorous, expert program evaluations on a regular basis—every two years—and ask if the service they are providing is having a meaningful input on the policy that informs it. Is the alignment between program and policy true? Again, we urge that this process be public, involving peers, experts and citizens. Web 2.0 technologies—building on blogs, wikis and as yet unknown communication and knowledge-gathering technologies—hold the potential to unleash citizen input into the design and nature of services. Customers—and citizens—today expect to be heard and the reality is that often they know far more than the service providers do about the nature and implications of a service. The service state must meet them halfway. Procedural rules must be clear and the policy-making process must be simple, fair and flexible.

Is the service being offered at the right cost? There has to be a better accounting of the real costs of services. Too often services are priced with a variety of costs that are only tenuously related, while at other times the cost of supporting bureaucracies remain buried elsewhere. *Citizens, clients* and *customers* should be apprised of the cost of the services they consume (whether they are compelled to do so or not). It goes without saying that in many cases, the services being offered by the state are done so in the name of the public good (e.g., drivers' licences are a mechanism that allows the state to monitor driving suitability and, to a certain degree, control risk). But such calculations may be useful in identifying value-added products where the state could charge more than the real cost of production, thereby reducing the financial burden of offering the wide gamut of services.

Are we championing change? How do we make room for experimentation? The answer, we think, will lie in creating political and bureaucratic spaces where the risks can be debated and agreed upon. Legislatures—not just governments—must sanction the temporary creation of new services or new approaches. It must suspend its promotion of one-size-fits-all approaches and be indulgent if the results anticipated are not delivered on schedule. Public service is not a business—it does not choose its customers. The creation of service, or the re-imagination of a public good, takes time, study and examination. At the same time, the public service must invest in providing crystal clear data and in being forthright in admitting both the failings and the successes of new approaches.

What is the benchmark for partnership? The question of partnership is delicate and governments have encumbered the process with all sorts of rules. Governments have been known to impose partnerships on public servants for political purposes. There should be only a few tests: Will this partnership lead to a better integration of service for the customer, the client or the citizen? Will this partnership lead to better efficiencies? Will the population be better served?

Addressing such questions in a meaningful manner—one that places front and centre the notion of the citizen at the heart of both service delivery and service design—requires a reframing of the apparatus of the service state and its key stakeholders, including public servants, politicians and the public at large. In short, a new narrative for a more networked and participative governance model is required.

The mappings of this new narrative have been provided by Gerry Stoker in his framing of public value management (PVM) as an alternative lens to those of its predecessors (and, in many ways, ongoing rivals): traditional public administration (TPA) and new public management (NPM). Although we introduced Stoker's PVM typology in chapter six as one well aligned with the advent of Web 2.0 (and thus beginning to reshape the service transformation discourse), Stoker's efforts certainly predate the Internet's latest version, and are indeed much less about technology than the overall ethos of the public sector and the roles and inter-relationships that result.

Stoker's comparison between TPA and NPM in terms of key objectives of the system, for instance, invokes tensions that have been particularly prevalent in Canada in recent years between spending scandals and new controls on the one hand, and the Citizens First-type emphasis on customer satisfaction on the other. Specifically, Stoker presents the objective of TPA as "services monitored through bureaucratic oversight", whereas in the case of NPM it is "managing inputs and outputs in a way that ensures economy and responsiveness to consumers" (Stoker 2004: 21). By contrast, a PVM-driven philosophy of governance and service dictates that "the overarching goal is achieving public value that in turn involves greater effectiveness in tackling problems that the public most cares about [and the result is that] it stretches from service delivery to service maintenance" (Stoker 2006: 44).

Consequently, the role of public servants shifts from one of managing the achievement of specific quantifiable targets to one of stewardship in devising networked mechanisms for both design and delivery in a manner that seeks to inject participative learning and innovation in a systemic manner (thus the shift from delivery to holistic maintenance). As Stoker underscores, such a model does not accept any one sector's monopoly on service provision (as NPM implies), but begins from the premise that a multitude of stakeholder arrangements are possible. Within such diversity, much of the important work of the public sector is participatory and conversational in character, nurturing shared value sets through complex interactions among governments, citizens and community-centred stakeholders.

Such reflections hark back to the television commercial produced by the Canada Revenue Agency and its depiction of individuals plucking tax credits from the air. Our vision of a service state would make that ad available on the CRA website as an easy reference point. The site would provide an easy-to-complete tax form where every tax credit would be presented to the citizen. The tax form would invite the citizen to respond to questions and then make a decision as to whether the person was entitled to this or that tax credit. A phone number would link the citizen with the CRA if a question proved too open to interpretation. The citizen would be enlightened by being educated and knowing. It is an example of how tax collection services can be designed to better meet the needs of the *customer*, but also to identify all the intended *clients* for its many legislated provisions. Ultimately, it will also serve the *citizen* by better informing him or her of the range of tax expenditures the state is willing to incur and the behaviours the state is attempting to encourage.

Furthermore, as is now beginning to occur, new dialogues can form both online and offline to spur collective innovation in terms of how information is gathered from different sources and processed—by a variety of stakeholders in unstructured and unanticipated ways—into value-creating knowledge and actions. To return once again to CRA's realm of taxation, a 2009 Accenture report on Web 2.0 in the public sector illustrates the differences between an electronic delivery focus shaped by customer and NPM-driven mindset versus one driven by the collaborative potential for Web 2.0 and PVM:

> With Web 2.0 capabilities, intelligence could be baked into the service (a live agent could be contacted in real time) to identify an individual's personal circumstances and the profile of previous returns and then start asking questions that would help the citizen to complete the tax return faster and more efficiently. These questions would also prompt a user to think about the life circumstances that might have changed in the 12 months since the last return (Accenture 2009: 15).

Finally, the taxation authority would itself be only one of many venues housing discussions and information sources on various aspects of financial planning. The potential for value from a citizen's perspective rests less in compliance with efficient delivery channels than with more effective, multi-faceted learning networks. These networks enable a greater empowerment of taxpayers (in terms of how they plan for and pay taxes), and greater input by taxpayers into the design and maintenance of the service apparatus, with important implications for further strengthening the feedback and adaptation loop between service and policy (i.e., what services are working well and not working well; how can they be improved; and what new services may be worthy of consideration).

This networked logic of participation and diversity is all the more crucial as one shifts from one specific realm, such as taxation, to the multi-dimensional agendas of socio-economic development that cross over both intra-governmental and inter-governmental boundaries. While service integrator Service Canada struggles to leverage its federal presence within a community in a manner that seeks not to crowd out provincial, municipal and non-governmental actors, the resulting discourse that is required cannot be housed solely, or even primarily, within the confines of Ottawa head-quarters and central agencies. Shackled between the confines of traditional public administration and the limited space granted to it for customer satisfaction (driven by an awkward mix of NPM objectives and more centralized, integrated mechanisms for service bundles), Service Canada has been unable to fulfil its potential as a catalyst for service innovation in a manner that pursues public value in a genuinely citizen-centric manner. The same could be said about its provincial counterparts.

Asking the right questions and working towards innovative solutions will keep public servants motivated to create their own culture of service. It is our view—one consistent with the networked narrative of PVM—that genuine *customer*, *client* and *citizen* input, combined with a receptive and agile public sector (including managers and elected officials) that is confident that it can experiment and take chances on improving and rein-venting service, can move us closer to a 21ˢᵗ century model of democratic governance and service provision that genuinely seeks and rewards service excellence. As the public sector reaches its limits in terms of the usage and adoption of a customer-centric apparatus—largely devised from central corridors with limited input from front-line workers, delivery partners and service recipients—the next generation of the service state, one more truly citizen-centric, awaits co-discovery and collective design.

BIBLIOGRAPHY

Accenture 2007. "Leadership in Customer Service – Delivering on the Promise." http://nstore.accenture.com/acn_com/PDF/2007LCSReport_DeliveringPromiseFinal.pdf.

Accenture 2009. "Web 2.0 and the Next Generation of Public Service." www.accenture.com/NR/rdonlyres/C70B1B86-E876-4A20-9CF1-5121ABB2668A/0/Accenture_Public_Service_Web_2_dot_0_in_Public_Service_3.pdf.

Adolfsson, P. and E. Wikstrom 2007. "After Quantification: Quality Dialogue and Performance." *Financial Accountability and Management*, 23: 1: 73–89.

Affisco, J. and K. Soliman 2006. "E-Government: A Strategic Operations Management Framework for Service Delivery." *Business Process Management Journal*, 12: 1: 13–21.

Agranoff, R. 2003. *Leveraging Networks: A Guide for Public Managers Working Across Organizations*. Report. Washington, DC: IBM Center for the Business of Government. www.businessofgovernment.org/main/publications/grant_reports/details/index.asp?GID=130.

Alberta 2005. *Southern Alberta Child and Youth Health Network – Evaluation Report*. Calgary, AB: Southern Alberta Child and Youth Health Network. www.sacyhn.ca/goals.php.

Alberta 2008. *2007 Corporate Employee Survey*. Edmonton, AB: Alberta Corporate Human Resources, Government of Alberta.

Allen, B. A. et al. 2005. "E-Government as Collaborative Governance: Structural, Accountability and Cultural Reform." In *Practicing E-Government: A Global Perspective*, ed. M. Khosrow-Pour. Hershey, PA: Ideas Group Publishing, 1–15, 364–382.

Ambrose, R., D. Lenihan and J. Milloy, eds. 2006. "Managing the Federation: A Citizen-Centred Approach." *The Crossing Boundaries Papers 7*. Ottawa: Crossing Boundaries National Council, 10–11.

Andison, S. 2004. *IT Procurement Chapter – E-BC Strategic Plan*. Final draft discussion document. www.cio.gov.bc.ca/ebc/discussion/SRmodel_ver7_Final.pdf.

Andrew, C. 2002. "What is the Municipal Potential?" Report. Regina, SK: Saskatchewan Institute of Public Policy.

Anonymous 2006 (November). "Stronger Public Services." *Canadian Government Executive*, 12–13.

Aucoin, P. 2002. "Beyond the "New" in Public Management Reform in Canada: Catching the Next Wave?" In *The Handbook of Canadian Public Administration*, ed. C. Dunn. Oxford, UK: Oxford University Press, 37–52.

Aucoin, P., J. Smith and G. Dinsdale 2004. "Responsible Government: Clarifying Essentials, Dispelling Myths and Exploring Change." Ottawa: Canada School of Public Service. www.csps-efpc.gc.ca/pbp/pub/pdfs/P120_e.pdf.

Australia 2004. AGIMO (Government Information Management Office). *Collective Accountability*. Report. Canberra, AU: Government of Australia.

Australia 2006. State of Victoria, Public Accounts and Estimates Committee. *Report on Private Investment in Public Infrastructure No. 240, Session 2003-06*. Melbourne, AU: Government Printer for the State of Victoria. www.parliament.vic.gov.au.

Baines, D. 2004. "Pro-market, non-market: the dual nature of organizational change in social services delivery." *Critical Social Policy*, 24: 1: 5–29.

Bakvis, H. 2000. "Rebuilding Policy Capacity in the Era of the Fiscal Dividend: A Report from Canada." *Governance*, 13: 1: 71–103.

Bakvis, H. and L. Juillet 2004. "The Horizontal Challenge: Line Departments, Central Agencies, and Leadership." Ottawa: Canada School of Public Service.

Bakvis, H. and G. Skogstad, eds. 2008. *Canadian Federalism: Performance, Effectiveness and Legitimacy*, 2nd edition. Toronto: Oxford University Press, 9.

Barnett, N. 2002. "Including ourselves: New Labour and engagement with public services." *Management Decision*, 40: 4: 310–317.

Barton, A. 2006. "Public Sector Accountability and Commercial-in-Confidence Outsourcing Contracts." *Accounting, Auditing and Accountability Journal*, 19: 2: 256–271.

Barzelay, M. with B. Armajani 1992. *Breaking through Bureaucracy: A New Vision for Managing in Government*. Berkeley: University of California Press.

Batini, C. et al. 2002. "Cooperative Architectures." In *Advances in Digital Government – Technology, Human Factors and Policy*, eds. W. J. McIver and A. K. Elmagarmid. Boston: Kluwer Academic Publishers, chapter 3.

Beierle, T. 2002. *Democracy Online: An Evaluation of the National Dialogue on Public Involvement in EPA Decisions*. Washington, DC: Resources for the Future. www.rff.org/rff/Documents/RFF-RPT-demonline.pdf.

Belanger, D., A. Coe and J. Roy 2007 (July 24). "Why Business Models Matter." *CIO Government Review*.

Belcourt, M. and S. Taggar 2002. "Making Government the Best Place to Work: Building Commitment." *New Directions – Number 8*. Toronto: Institute of Public Administration of Canada. http://unpan1.un.org/intradoc/groups/public/documents/IPAC/UNPAN012528.pdf.

Bellamy, C., 6 Perri and C. Raab 2005. "Joined Up Government and Privacy in the United Kingdom: Managing Tensions Between Data Protection and Social Policy. Part II." *Public Administration Review*, 83: 2: 395–415.

Bent, S., K. Kernaghan and D. B. Marson 1999. *Innovations and Good Practices in Single-Window Service.* Report. Ottawa: Canadian Centre for Management Development, March. http://dsp-psd.pwgsc.gc.ca/Collection/SC94-70-1999E.pdf.

Bevir, M., R. Rhodes and P. Weller 2003. "Traditions of Governance: Interpreting the Changing Role of the Public Sector." *Public Administration Review*, 81: 1: 1–17.

Biddle, B. J. and M. M. Marlin 1987. "Causality, Confirmation, Credulity, and Structural Equation Modeling." *Child Development*, 58: 1: 4–17.

Blair, Rt. Hon. T. 2006. "21st Century Public Services." *Speech to the Public Services Reform Conference*, 2006, June 6, London, UK. www.number10.gov.uk/output/page9564.asp.

Blakemore M. 2006. "Think Paper 2: Customer-centric, citizen-centric. Should Government learn directly from business? Version No. 5.0." Prepared for the eGovernment unit, DG Information Society and Media, European Commission, October 24, Brussels, Belgium. http://europa.eu.int/egovernment_research.

Borins, S. 2000. "Trends in Training Public Managers." *International Public Management Journal*, 2: 2a: 229–314.

Borins, S. 2004. "A Holistic View of Public Sector Information Technology." *Journal of E-Government*, 1: 2: 3–29.

Borins, S. et al. 2007. *The Digital State at the Leading Edge.* Toronto: University of Toronto Press.

Bouchard, G. 1991. "Les relations fonctionnaires-citoyens: un cadre d'analyse." *Canadian Public Administration*, 34: 4: 604–620.

Bouckaert, G. 2001. "Pride and Performance in Public Service: Some Patterns of Analysis." *International Review of Administrative Sciences*, 67: 1: 15–27.

Bouckaert, G. and S. Van de Walle 2003. "Comparing Measures of Citizen Trust and User Satisfaction as Indicators of 'Good Governance': Difficulties in Linking Trust and Satisfaction Indicators." *International Review of Administrative Sciences*, 69: 1: 329–43.

Bourgault, J. and M. Gusella 2001. "Performance, Pride and Recognition in the Canadian Federal Civil Service." *International Review of Administrative Sciences*, 67: 1: 29–47.

Brewer, G., S. C. Selden and R. L. Facer 2000. "Individual Conceptions of Public Service Motivation." *Public Administration Review*, 60: 3: 254–264.

British Columbia 2002–03. Office of the Auditor-General (BCA-G). *Building a Strong Work Environment in British Columbia's Public Service: A Key to Delivering Quality Service.* Victoria, BC: Queen's Printer of British Columbia, Report 2002–03: 1.

British Columbia 2004–05. Office of the Auditor-General (BCA-G). *Building a Strong Public Service: Reassessing the Quality of the Work Environment in British Columbia's Public Service.* Victoria, BC: Queen's Printer of British Columbia.

www.bcauditor.com/files/publications/2005/report10/report/building-strong-public-service.pdf.

British Columbia 2006a (August 18). Service BC. *Project Charter SBC-GA Training Orientation Project*. Victoria, BC: Ministry of Labour and Citizens' Services.

British Columbia 2006b. Service BC. *Service BC Project Summary Report*. Victoria, BC: Ministry of Labour and Citizens' Services. www.lcs.gov.bc.ca/asd/docs/Service_BC_Project_Summary.pdf.

British Columbia 2007a. (BCPSA) British Columbia Public Service Agency. *Annual Report*. Victoria, BC: British Columbia Public Service Agency.

British Columbia 2007b. Service BC. "Service BC Project." *Alliance Management Office Report*. Victoria, BC: Ministry of Labour and Citizens' Services. www.lcs.gov.bc.ca/asd/docs/48988_Service_BC_Project_AMO_Report_August_2007_(final).pdf.

British Columbia 2008a. BC Stats. "Public Sector Service Value Chain: Linking Employee Engagement & Customer Satisfaction." Victoria, BC: BC Stats, i, 12. www.bcstats.gov.bc.ca/data/ssa/reports/WES/WES2008-EmployeeCustomerLink.pdf.

British Columbia 2008b. Service BC Project. *Alliance Management Office Report*, Victoria, BC: Ministry of Labour and Citizens' Services. http://www.lcs.gov.bc.ca/asd/docs/ServiceBC_Report_report_Aug08.pdf.

British Columbia 2009a. Community Living BC. "Community Living BC, 3 Year Strategic Plan: 2009/2010 – 2011/2012." Victoria, BC: Ministry of Children and Family Development. www.communitylivingbc.ca/policies_and_publications/documents/CLBCStrategicPlan.pdf.

British Columbia 2009b. Online Channel Office. *Alliance Management Office Report*. Victoria, BC: Ministry of Labour and Citizens' Services. www.lcs.gov.bc.ca/asd/docs/ServiceBC_Report_report_Aug09.pdf.

Brown, D. 2006. "Inland revenue's ASPIRE procurement experience." *The Outsourcing Project – Achieving Competitive Advantage Through Collaborative Partnerships*. London, UK: CxO Research, 4: 1. www.cxolessons.com/documents.asp?d_ID=99.

Cameron, D. and R. Simeon 2002. "Intergovernmental Relations in Canada: The Emergence of Collaborative Federalism." *Publius*, 32: 2: 49–71.

Canada 2003. Government On-Line Advisory Panel. *Connecting With Canadians: Pursuing Service Transformation*. Ottawa: Treasury Board Secretariat. www.gol-ged.gc.ca/pnl-grp/reports/rep-rap-eng.asp.

Canada 2004. Public Works and Government Services Canada (PWGSC). "Government Wide Review of Procurement – Concepts for Discussion." *Parliamentary Secretary Task Force Report*. Ottawa: Government of Canada. Available at www.mmi-igm.ca/download/resources/ParliamentaryTaskForce_E.pdf.

Canada 2005a. Canada Public Service Agency. "Public service employees are strongly committed to their work." *Public Service Employee Survey, Survey Results*.

Ottawa: Government of Canada. www.psagency-agencefp.gc.ca/arc/survey-sondage/2005/r-publications/survey_e.asp#ToC_3.

Canada 2005b. "Government On-Line 2005 – From Vision to Reality and Beyond." *GOL Annual Report*. Ottawa: Treasury Board Secretariat. www.gol-ged.gc.ca.

Canada 2006a. *From Red Tape to Clear Results: The Report of the Blue Ribbon Panel on the Grants and Contributions Programs*. Ottawa: Government of Canada. http://dsp-psd.pwgsc.gc.ca/Collection/BT22-109-2007E.pdf.

Canada 2006b. Office of the Auditor-General (OAG). *Large Information Technology Projects*. Report. Ottawa: Office of the Auditor-General, chapter 3. www.oag-bvg.gc.ca.

Canada 2008a. Treasury Board of Canada. *Highlights on Results of the 2008 Public Service Employee Survey, Results on employee engagement*. Report. Ottawa: Government of Canada. www.tbs-sct.gc.ca/pses-saff/2008/highl-faits-eng.asp#sec.04.

Canada 2008b. Service Canada College. "Service Canada College and the Service Excellence Certification Program: Spearheading the Professionalization of the Service Delivery Function in Government." *CAPAM Award Submission*. Ottawa: Treasury Board of Canada.

Carlitz, R. and R. Gunn 2005. "E-rulemaking: a New Avenue for Public Engagement." *Journal of Public Deliberation*, 1: 1: article 7. http://services.be-press.com/cgi/viewcontent.cgi?article=1008&context=jpd

Carroll, B. W. and D. Siegel 1999. *Service in the Field*. Montreal, QC and Kingston, ON: McGill-Queen's University Press.

Carson, K. D. et al. 1999. "Four Commitment Profiles and their Relationships to Empowerment, Service Recovery and Work Attitudes." *Public Personnel Management*, 28: 1: 1–13.

CCMD 1999. *Citizen Centred Service: Responding to the Needs of Canadians*. Ottawa: Canadian Centre for Management Development (CCMD). www.iccs-isac.org/en/pubs/CCHandbook.pdf.

Charih, M. and J. Robert 2004. "Government Online in the Federal Government of Canada: The Organizational Issues." *International Review of Administrative Sciences*, 70: 2: 373–384.

Cherny, A. 2000. *The Next Deal – The Future of Public Life in the Information Age*. New York: Basic Books.

Clark, D. 2002. "Neoliberalism and Public Service Reform: Canada in Comparative Perspective." *Canadian Journal of Political Science*, 35: 4: 771–793.

Clarke, M. 1998. "The Challenges Facing Public Service Training Institutions." *International Review of Administrative Sciences*, 64: 3: 399–407.

Coble-Vinzant, J. and L. Crothers 1998. *Street-level leadership: discretion and legitimacy in front-line public service*. Washington, DC: Georgetown University Press.

Coe, A. 2004. "Government Online in Canada: Innovation and Accountability in 21st Century Government." Graduate research paper, Kennedy School of Government.

Coe, A., G. Paquet and J. Roy 2001. "E-Governance and Smart Communities: A Social Learning Challenge." *Social Science Computer Review*, 19: 1: 80–93.

Cole, J. 2008 (July 28). "Want to Know the Best Place to Work in Canada's Federal Public Service?" *Hill Times* (Ottawa), 28.

Coleman, S. and J. Gøtze 2003. *Bowling Together: Online Public Engagement in Policy Deliberation*. London, UK: Hansard Society.

Considine, M. 2001. *Enterprising States: The Public Management of Welfare-to-Work*. Cambridge, UK: Cambridge University Press.

Considine, M. 2002. "The end of the line? Accountable governance in the age of networks, partnerships and joined-up services." *Governance*, 15: 1: 21–40.

Considine, M. and J. Lewis 2003. "Bureaucracy, Network or Enterprise? Comparing Models of Governance in Australia, Britain, the Netherlands and New Zealand." *Public Administration Review*, 63: 2: 131–40.

Cresswell, A., G. Burke and A. Pardo 2006. *Advancing Return on Investment Analysis for Government IT*. Albany, NY: SUNY, Center for Technology in Government.

Crewson, P. E. 1997. "Public Service Motivation: Building Empirical Evidence of Incidence and Effect." *Journal of Public Administration Research and Theory*, 7: 4: 499–518.

Cross, M. 2007 January 18. "Joined-up Government is Not Inevitable or Desirable." *The Guardian* (London, UK), Technology. www.guardian.co.uk/technology/2007/jan/18/comment.society.

Curtin, G., M. H. Sommer and V. Vis-Sommer, eds. 2003. *The World of E-Government*. New York: Haworth Press.

Cutler, T., B. Waine and K. Brevony 2007. "A New Epoch of Individualization? Problems with the 'Personalization' of Public Sector Services." *Public Administration Review*, 85: 3: 847–55.

Das, H. M. D. and F. McKenzie 1995. "Assessing the Will of the People: An Investigation into Town Service Delivery Satisfaction." *Canadian Public Administration*, 38: 1: 77–93.

Deloitte Research 2008. "Change your world or the world will change you: the future of collaborative government and Web 2.0." www.deloitte.com/assets/Dcom-Canada/Local%20Assets/Documents/ca_govt_web20_mar08_EN.pdf.

Denis, C. 1995. "Government Can Do Whatever It Wants: Moral Regulation in Ralph Klein's Alberta." *The Canadian Review of Sociology and Anthropology*, 32: 3: 365–383.

Dobrowolsky, A. 1998. "Of 'Special Interest': Interest, Identity and Feminist Constitutional Activism in Canada." *Canadian Journal of Political Science*, 31: 4: 707–742.

Dryzek, J. 1982. "Policy Analysis as a Hermeneutic Activity." *Policy Sciences*, 14: 309–29.

du Gay, P. 2000. *In Praise of Bureaucracy: Weber/Organization/Ethics*. London, UK: Sage.

Dunleavy, P. et al. 2006. "New public management is dead. Long live digital-era governance." *Journal of Public Administration Research and Theory*, 16: 3: 467–494.

Dutil, P., J. Langford and J. Roy 2005. "Managing Service Transformation Relationships Between Government and Industry: Best Practices." *New Directions – Number 17*. Toronto: Institute of Public Administration of Canada.

Dutil, P., J. Langford and J. Roy 2007. "Rethinking Government-Public Relationships in a Digital World: Customers, Clients or Citizens?" *Journal of Information Technology and Politics*, 4: 1: 77–90.

Dutton, W. and M. Peitu 2007. *Reconfiguring Government-Public Engagements: Enhancing the Communicative Power of Citizens*. Oxford, UK: Oxford Internet Institute.

Dwivedi, O. P. and J. I. Gow 1999. *From Bureaucracy to Public Management*. Peterborough: Broadview.

Economist Intelligence Unit 2006. "Foresight 2020 – Economic, industry and corporate trends." Available at www.cisco.com/web/CA/pdf/ Cisco_Foresight_2020_Full_Report.pdf.

Edelman, M. 2006. "The Annual Edelman Trust Barometer." www.edelman.com/image/insights/content/FullSupplement_final.pdf.

Eggers, W. 2005. *Government 2.0: Using Technology to Improve Education, Cut Red Tape, Reduce Gridlock and Enhance Democracy*. New York: Rowman and Littlefield Publishers.

Ekos Research Associates 2006. *Service Canada: Awareness Baseline Study Final Report*. Prepared for Service Canada, Government of Canada. Available at www.servicecanada.gc.ca/eng/about/por/awareness/index.shtml.

Entwistle, T. and S. Martin 2005. "From Competition to Collaboration in Public Service Delivery: A New Agenda for Research." *Public Administration Review*, 83: 1: 233–242.

Erin Research Inc. 1998. *Citizens First*. Survey. Ottawa: Canadian Centre for Management Development.

Erin Research Inc. 2000. *Citizens First 2000*. Survey. Toronto: Institute of Public Administration of Canada.

Erin Research Inc. 2003. *Citizens First 3*. Survey. Toronto: Institute of Public Administration of Canada.

Erin Research Inc. 2008. *Citizens First 5*. Survey. Toronto: Institute for Citizen-Centred Service.

Evers, A. 2005. "Mixed Welfare Systems and Hybrid Organizations: Changes in the Governance and Provision of Social Services." *International Journal of Public Administration*, 29: 9–10: 737–748.

Farley, J. M. 1993. "Surveys–Vital Elements of Customer Service." In *Creating a Customer-focused Organization/Report 1030*, eds. T. Brothers and K. Carson. Selected speeches given at the Conference Board's Creating and Maintaining Customer-Focused Organizations Conference, New York City, June 9-10, 1992.

Fitzgerald, M. R. and R. F. Durant 1980. "Citizen Evaluations and Urban Management: Service Delivery in an Era of Protest." *Public Administration Review*, 40: 6: 585–594.

Fleming, J. and J. Asplund 2007. *Human Sigma: Managing the Employee-Customer Encounter.* New York: Gallup Press.

Flinders, M. 2005. "The politics of public-private partnerships." *British Journal of Politics and International Relations*, 7: 2: 215–239.

Flumian, M., A. Coe and K. Kernaghan 2007. "Transforming Service to Canadians: The Service Canada Model." *International Review of Administrative Sciences*, 73: 4: 557–568.

Foster, P. and P. Wilding 2000. "Whither Welfare Professionalism?" *Social Policy and Administration*, 34: 2: 143–159

Fountain, J. E. 2001. *Building the Virtual State: Information Technology and Institutional Change.* Washington, DC: Brookings Institution Press.

Fowler, F. J. 2002. *Survey Research Methods,* 3rd edition. Thousand Oaks, CA: Sage.

Fox, G. and D. Lenihan 2006. "Where Does the Buck Stop? Accountability and Joint Initiatives." Ottawa: Public Policy Forum and Crossing Boundaries National Council. www.ppforum.ca/common/assets/reports/en/accountability_and_joint_initiatives.pdf.

Gallup Consulting 2008. "Employee Engagement: What's Your Engagement Ratio?" Survey. www.gallup.com/consulting/121535/Employee-Engagement-Overview-Brochure.aspx.

Gartner Inc. 2007. "What Does Web 2.0 Mean to Government?" Stamford, CT: Gartner Inc., No. G00146261. www.rapidhost.ru/kart/users/user164/File/what_does_web_20_mean_to_gov_146261.pdf.

Gates, Bill 2006. Speech to the *Microsoft Government Leaders Forum Europe*, February 1, 2006. www.microsoft.com/presspass/exec/billg/speeches/2006/02-01GLFEurope.mspx.

Gibbons, R. 2004. "Federalism and the Challenge of Electronic Portals." In *E-Government Reconsidered: Renewal of Governance for the Knowledge Age*, eds. L. Oliver and L. Sanders. Regina: Canadian Plains Research Center, chapter 2.

Goldsmith, S. and W. D. Eggers 2004. *Governing by Networks – the New Shape of the Public Sector.* Washington, DC: Brookings Institution Press.

Goodin, R. E. 2003. "Democratic Accountability: The Third Sector and All." Working paper no. 19. Cambridge, MA: Harvard University, The Hauser Centre for Nonprofit Organizations. Available at http://papers.ssrn.com/sol3/papers.cfm?abstract_id=418262.

Goodsell, C. T. 1994. *The Case for Bureaucracy: A Public Administration Polemic.* Chatham, NY: Chatham House Publishers Inc.

Gow, I. 2004. *A Canadian model of Public Administration?* Research paper. Ottawa: Canada School of Public Service. www.csps-efpc.gc.ca/pbp/pub/pdfs/p121_e.pdf.

Griffiths, J. M. 2001. "Real-time bandwidth renegotiation through learnt behaviour." *International Journal of Communications Systems*, 14: 6: 549–560.

Gronlund, A., ed. 2002. *E-government — Design, Applications and Management.* Hershey, PA: Ideas Group Publishing.

Guan, L. 2008 (April 8). "Web 2.0: Knowledge frontier for organisations." Published online at CRN: Connecting the Australian Channel. www.crn.com.au/News/107686,web-20-knowledge-frontier-for-organisations.aspx.

Halvorson, J. and M. Rodrigues 1996. "City of Mississauga Presentation to the Commonwealth Association for Public Administration and Management." Mississauga, ON, 14.

Hamel, G. and B. Breen 2007. *The Future of Management.* Cambridge, MA: Harvard Business School Press.

Hammersley, M. 2005. 'Should Social Science Be Critical?' *Philosophy of the Social Sciences*, 35: 2: 175–195.

Hardina, D. 2005. "Ten Characteristics of Empowerment-Oriented Social Service Organizations." *Administration in Social Work*, 29: 3: 23–42.

Hart-Teeter Research 2003. *The New è-Government Equation: Ease, Engagement, Privacy and Protection.* Research for the Council for Excellence in Government and Accenture. www.excelgov.org/usermedia/images/uploads/PDFs/egovpoll2003.pdf.

Hay Group Insight 2006. *Saskatchewan Public Service 2005 Employee Survey: Government-wide Results.* Regina: Saskatchewan Public Service. www.psc.gov.sk.ca/Default.aspx?DN=2cfaa73c-829d-48c4-9745-e5c1c3911c2a&Anc=2cfaa73c-829d-48c4-9745-e5c1c3911c2a&Pa=04eb8156-33be-46e7-956c-8d6556ccc5c9.

Heintzman, R. and B. Marson 2005. "People, Service and Trust: Is there a Public Sector Service Value Chain?" *International Review of Administrative Sciences*, 71: 4: 549–575.

Henman, P. and M. Adler 2003. "Information Technology and the Governance of Social Security." *Critical Social Policy*, 23: 2: 139–164.

Hickey, S. 1996. "Continuous Learning." *Presentation made to the Commonwealth Association for Public Administration and Management (CAPAM).*

Hodge, G. A. 2004. "The risky business of public-private partnerships." *Australian Journal of Public Administration*, 63: 4: 37–49.

Hodge, G. A. and K. Coghill 2004. *Governing the Privatized State: The Accountability Challenge.* Department of Management Working Paper Series. Melbourne, AU:

Monash University. www.buseco.monash.edu.au/mgt/research/working-papers/2004/wp57-04.pdf.

Hoggett, P., C. Miller and M. Mayo 2007. "Individualization and Ethical Agency." In *Contested Individualization: Debates about Contemporary Personhood*, ed. C. Howard. New York: Palgrave Macmillan, chapter 6.

Hood, C. 1991. "A Public Management for all Seasons?" *Public Administration Review*, 69: 1: 3–19.

Howard, C. 2003. "The Promise and Performance of Mutual Obligation." In *Neoliberalism and the Australian Welfare State*, ed. C. Aspalter. Taiwan: Casa Verde Publishing, chapter 7.

Howard, C. 2006. "The new governance of Australian welfare: street-level contingencies." In *Administering Welfare Reform: International transformations in welfare governance*, eds. P. Henman and M. Fenger. Bristol, UK: The Policy Press, University of Bristol, chapter 7.

Hubberstey, C. 2001. "Client Involvement as a Key Element of Integrated Case Management." *Child & Youth Care Forum*, 30: 2: 83–97.

Hume, D. 2006. *From the System to the Citizen: New Directions in Democratic Renewal*. Ottawa: Crossing Boundaries National Council. www.crossingboundaries.ca/files/kta_vol6.pdf.

Hupe, P. and M. Hill 2007. "Street Level Bureaucracy and Public Accountability." *Public Administration Review*, 85: 2: 279–299.

Hutton, J. 2006. "Speech by John Hutton, Secretary of State for Work and Pensions." www.nationalschool.gov.uk/psrc2006/downloads/speech_john_hutton.pdf.

IATF 2007. *A Pan-Canadian Framework for Identity Management and Authentication*. Interim report. Ottawa: Inter-jurisdictional Identity Management and Authentication Task Force. Available at www.cio.gov.bc.ca/local/cio/idim/documents/iatf.pdf.

ICCS 2003. *Integrated Service Delivery: A Critical Analysis*. Report sponsored by the Public Sector Service Delivery Council. Toronto: Institute for Citizen-Centred Service. www.iccs-isac.org.

ICCS 2008a. "About the Institute." Toronto: Institute for Citizen-Centred Service. www.iccs-isac.org/eng/about.htm.

ICCS 2008b. "About the Common Measurements Tool." Toronto: Institute for Citizen-Centred Service. www.iccs-isac.org/eng/cmt-about.htm.

ICCS 2008c. "Request CMT." Toronto: Institute for Citizen-Centred Service. www.iccs-isac.org/eng/RequestCMT.htm.

ICCS 2008d. "Innovative Citizen-Centred Services through Collaboration." Toronto: Institute for Citizen-Centred Service. www.iccs-isac.org/eng/Event_Materials/CAPAM%202006/ICCS%20Overview%20and%20Services.pdf.

Ipsos-Reid 2007. "OPS Employee Survey." *Ontario Public Service Overall Report* for the Ontario Public Service. Toronto: Queen's Printer for Ontario.

ITAC 2004. "Task Force on Large IT Projects." *Presentation to the Government of Ontario Sponsored Review Panel.* Ottawa: Information Technology Association of Canada. www.itac.ca.

Johns, C. M., P. L. O'Reilly and G. J. Inwood 2007. "Formal and Informal Dimensions of Intergovernmental Administrative Relations in Canada." *Canadian Public Administration* 50: 1: 21–41.

Johnson, B. 2005. *Strategies for Successful Joined Up Government Initiatives.* Perth, AU: John Curtin Institute of Public Policy, Institute of Public Administration of Australia, Department of Premier and Cabinet.

Jurkiewicz, C. et al. 1998. "Motivation in Public and Private Organizations: A Comparative Study." *Public Productivity & Management Review,* 21: 3: 230–250.

Kabachnik, T. 2006. *I Quit, But Forgot to Tell You.* Largo, FL: The Kabachnick Group.

Kamarck, E. C. 2004. *Applying 21ˢᵗ-Century Government to the Challenge of Homeland Security.* Washington, DC: IBM Center for the Business of Government.

Kamensky, J. M. and T. Burlin, eds. 2004. *Collaboration – Using Networks and Partnerships.* IBM Center for The Business of Government Book Series. Lanham, MD: Rowman and Littlefield Publishers Inc.

Kampen, J. K. 2007. "The Impact of Survey Methodology and Context on Central Tendency, Nonresponse and Associations of Subjective Indicators of Government Performance." *Quality & Quantity,* 41: 2: 793–813.

Kanter, R. 1991. "Even Closer to the Customer." *Harvard Business Review,* 69: 1: 9–10.

Kearsey, A. and R. J. Varey 1998. "Managerialist Thinking on Marketing for Public Services." *Public Money and Management,* 18: 2: 51–60.

Kelly, J. M. and D. Swindell 2002. "A Multiple-Indicator Approach to Municipal Service Evaluation: Correlating Performance Measurement and Citizen Satisfaction across Jurisdictions." *Public Administration Review,* 62: 5: 610–21.

Kernaghan, K. 1991. "Career Public Service 2000: Road to Renewal or Impractical Vision?" *Canadian Public Administration,* 34: 4: 551–572.

Kernaghan, K. 1992. "Empowerment and Public Administration: Revolutionary Advance or Passing Fancy?" *Canadian Public Administration,* 35: 2: 194–214.

Kernaghan, K. 2000. "The Post Bureaucratic Organization and Public Service Values." *International Review of Administrative Science,* 66: 1: 91–104.

Kernaghan, K. 2005. "Moving toward the virtual state: Integrating services and service channels for citizen-centred service." *International Review of Administrative Sciences,* 71: 1: 119–131.

Kernaghan, K. 2008. *Integrating Service Delivery: Barriers and Benchmarks.* Toronto: Institute for Citizen Centred Service. Available at http://networkedgovernment.ca/cp.asp?pid=992.

Kernaghan, K. and J. Gunraj 2004. "Integrating Information Technology into Public Administration: Conceptual and Practical Considerations." *Canadian Public Administration*, 47: 4: 525–546.

Kernaghan K. and J. Langford 1990. *The Responsible Public Servant*. Toronto: Institute of Public Administration of Canada.

Kettl, D. F. 1993. "Review of M. Barzelay's 'Breaking Through Bureaucracy'." *American Political Science Review*, 87: 3: 786–787.

Kettl, D. F. 2005. *The Next Government of the United States: Challenges for Performance in the 21ˢᵗ Century*. Washington, DC: IBM Center for the Business of Government.

Keiningham, T. et al. 2005. *Loyalty Myths*. Hoboken, NJ: John Wiley & Sons.

Lacasse, R. 1991. "Leadership and the creation of a service culture." *Canadian Public Administration*, 34: 3: 474–489.

Langford, J. 2008. "Service Transformation in a Citizen-Centric World." *Optimumonline* [electronic journal], 38: 1: 5–11. www.optimumonline.ca/article.phtml?id=298.

Langford, J. and Y. Harrison 2001. "Partnering for e-government: challenges for public administrators." *Canadian Public Administration*, 44: 4: 393–416.

Langford, J., R. MacDonald and D. Taschereau-Mamers, forthcoming. "Service B.C.: Building Citizen-Centred Service Delivery in B.C." Case study conducted in 2007–2008 and revised in 2010. Victoria, BC: Service BC.

Langford, J. and J. Roy 2006a. "E-Government and Public-Private Partnerships in Canada: When Failure is No Longer an Option." *International Journal of Electronic Business*, 4: 2: 118–135.

Langford, J. and J. Roy 2006b. "E-Government, Service Transformation & Procurement Reform: The Evolution of Industry – Government Relations in Canada." In *The Encyclopedia of Digital Government*, ed. A. Anttiroiko. London, UK: Idea Group Reference, vol II: 595.

Langford, J. and J. Roy 2008a. "Service Transformation and Public-Private IT Partnerships: Moving Towards Shared Accountability." *International Journal of Public Policy*, 4: 3-4: 232–250.

Langford, J. and J. Roy 2008b. *Integrating Service Delivery across Levels of Government: Case Studies of Canada and Other Countries*. Washington, DC: IBM Center for the Business of Government, Collaboration: Networks and Partnership Series. Available at www.grandsorganismes.gouv.qc.ca/app/DocRepository/1/Rond_Point/RoyLangfordReport.pdf

Law, J. and J. Urry 2004. "Enacting the social." *Economy and Society*, 33: 3: 390–410.

Lawther, W. 2002. *Contracting for the 21ˢᵗ Century: A Partnership Model*. Washington, DC: PricewaterhouseCoopers Endowment for The Business of Government.

Lenihan, D., ed. 2007. *Transformational Changes and Policy Shifts in Support of Partnerships – Within, Across and Outside of Government*. Ottawa: Crossing Boundaries National Council.

Leisink, P. and B. Steijn 2009. "Public Service Motivation and Job Performance of Public Sector Employees in the Netherlands" *International Review of Administrative Sciences*, 75: 1: 35–53.

Leon, A. M. 1999. "Family support model: integrating service delivery in the twenty-first century" *Families in Society*, 80: 1: 14-24.

Lindquist, E. 2004. "Strategy, Capacity and Horizontal Government: Perspectives from Australia and Canada." *Optimumonline* [electronic journal], 34: 4: 2. www.optimumonline.ca/article.phtml?e=mesokurj&id=212.

Lipsky, M. 1980. *Street Level Bureaucracy: Dilemmas of the Individual in Public Service*. New York: Russell Sage Foundation.

Lukensmeyer, C. and L. Torres 2006. *Public Deliberation: A Manager's Guide to Citizen Engagement*. Washington, DC: IBM Center of the Business of Government. www.businessofgovernment.org/pdfs/LukensmeyerReport.pdfIPAC/RRSP.

Lyons, S. T., L. Duxbury and C. Higgins 2006. "A Comparison of the Values and Commitment of Private Sector, Public Sector and Parapublic Sector Employees." *Public Administration Review*, 86: 4: 605–618.

MacDonald, M. and G. MacDonald 2003. "Using Strategy to Focus the Results of Knowledge Management." *Canadian Government Executive*, January: 12–14.

Mandell, M. 2005 (Summer). *The Impact of Changing Expectations in Complex Networks*. www.csus.edu/ccp/newsletter/2005/Summer/#challengingissue. This article is based in part on: R. Keast, M. P. Mandell, K. Brown and G. Woolcock 2004. "Network Structures: Working Differently and Changing Expectations." *Public Administration Review*, 64: 3.

Manitoba 2005. *Manitoba Civil Service Employee Opinion Survey: Results Report*. Winnipeg, MB: Government of Manitoba, Spring 2005.

Marson, B. 1991 (Spring). "Government as a Service Enterprise." *Public Sector Management, IPAC*. Toronto: Institute of Public Administration Canada, 12–14.

Maynard-Moody, S. and M. Musheno 2003. *Cops, Teachers, Counselors: Stories from the Front Lines of Public Service*. Ann Arbor: University of Michigan Press, 93–94.

McCoach, D. B., A. C. Black and A. A. O'Connell 2007. "Errors of Inference in Structural Equation Modeling." *Psychology in the Schools*, 44: 5: 461–470.

McIntosh, T. 2004. "Intergovernmental relations, social policy and federal transfers after Romanow." *Canadian Public Administration*, 47: 1: 27–51.

McKevitt, D., M. Millar and J. Keogan 2000. "The Role of the Citizen-Client in Performance Measurement: The Case of the Street Level Public Organization." *International Review of Administrative Sciences*, 66: 2: 619–636.

McLennan, J. D et al. 2003. *The Integration of Health and Social Services for Young Children and Their Families.* Ottawa: Canadian Health Services Research Foundation.

Metzenbaum, S. 2006. *Performance Accountability: The Five Building Blocks and Six Essential Practices.* Washington, DC: IBM Center for the Business of Government.

Miles, J. and M. Shelvin 2001. *Applying Regression & Correlation: A Guide for Students and Researchers.* London, UK: Sage.

Milward, H. B. and K. G. Provan 2006. *A Manager's Guide to Choosing and Using Collaborative Networks.* Washington, DC: IBM Center for the Business of Government.

Moe, R.C. 2001. "The Emerging Quasi-Federal Government: Issues of Management and Accountability." *Public Administration Review*, 61: 1: 290–312.

Morin, B. 1992. "Pour une meilleure qualité du service aux citoyens: déconcentration et imputabilité." *Canadian Public Administration*, 35: 2: 181–193.

Moule, L. 2007 (June 5). "Rescuing the Lost Citizen." *CIO Government Review.* www.itworldcanada.com/news/find-a-government-service-with-econtact-rescuing-the-lost-citizen/01089.

Mulgan, R. 2003. "Centrelink - A New Approach To Welfare Service Delivery?" In *Neoliberalism and the Australian Welfare State,* ed. C. Aspalter. Hong Kong: Casa Verde, chapter 9.

New Brunswick 2007 (May–June). "Public Service Employee Survey – Summary Report." Fredericton: Government of New Brunswick, 12. www.gnb.ca/0163/Summary_Report-e.pdf.

New Zealand 2000. *E-government: A Vision for New Zealanders.* Wellington, NZ: Government of New Zealand. www.e.govt.nz/about-egovt/vision.html.

New Zealand 2007. *New Zealand E-government 2007: Progress Towards Transformation.* Auckland, NZ: Government of New Zealand, chapter 6. www.e.govt.nz/resources/research/progress/agency-initiatives/chapter6.html.

Norris, P. 2003. "Will New Technology Boost Turnout? Experiments in e-Voting and All-Postal Voting in British Local Elections." Paper prepared for the *British Study Group Seminar*, Minda de Gunzberg Center for European Studies, Harvard University.

Northwest Territories 2008. NWT Bureau of Statistics. *2008 Employee Satisfaction and Engagement Survey.* Yellowknife, NT: Government of the Northwest Territories.

Nova Scotia 2005. Nova Scotia Public Service Commission. *"How's Work Going?" 2005 Employee Survey Results.* Halifax, NS: Crown Copyright.

Nova Scotia 2007. Nova Scotia Public Service Commission. *"How's Work Going?" Nova Scotia Employee Survey Results.* Halifax, NS: Crown Copyright.

Nutley, S. M., I. Walter and H. T. O. Davies 2007. *Using Evidence: How research can inform public services.* Bristol, UK: Policy Press.

OECD 2001 (March). "The Hidden Threat to E-Government, Avoiding Large Government IT Failures." *PUMA Policy Brief no.* 8. Paris: Organisation for Economic Co-operation and Development. www.oecd.org/dataoecd/46/6/35064033.pdf.

OECD 2002. *Territorial Review of Canada.* Paris: Organisation for Economic Co-operation and Development. www.oecdbookshop.org/oecd/display.asp?lang =EN&sf1=identifiers&st1=9789264198326.

OECD 2003 (March). "The E-Government Imperative." Policy brief. *OECD Observer.* Paris: Organisation for Economic Co-operation and Development. www.oecd.org/dataoecd/60/60/2502539.pdf.

O'Flynn, J. and J. Wanna 2008. *Collaborative Governance: A New Era of Public Policy in Australia.* Canberra: ANU E Press.

Osborne, D. and T. Gaebler 1992. *Reinventing Government.* Reading, MA: Addison-Wesley.

Paquet, G. 1997. "States, Communities and Markets: The Distributed Governance Scenario." In *The Nation-State in a Global Information Era: Policy Challenges,* ed. T. J. Courchene. The Bell Canada Papers in *Economics and Public Policy,* 5. Kingston, ON: John Deutsch Institute for the Study of Economic Policy, 25–46.

Paquet, G. 2004. "There is More to Governance than Public Candelabras: E-governance and Canada's Public Service." In *E-Government Reconsidered: Renewal of Governance for the Knowledge Age,* eds. L. Oliver, and L. Sanders. Regina: Canadian Plains Research Center.

Paquet, G. and J. Roy 2004. "Smarter Cities in Canada." *Optimumonline* [electronic journal], 33: 1: 2–20.

Pardo, T. and L. Dadayan 2006 (September). "Service New Brunswick." Case study. Albany, NY: State University at Albany, Center for Technology in Government, Public ROI – Advancing Return on Investment Series. www.ctg.albany.edu/publications/reports/proi_case_service.

Parker, S. and N. Gallagher, eds. 2007. *The Collaborative State: How Working Together Can Transform Public Services.* London, UK: Demos.

Parks, R. B. 1984. "Linking Objective and Subjective Measures of Performance." *Public Administration Review,* 44: 2, 118–127.

Pegnato, J. A. 1997. "Is a Citizen a Customer?" *Public Productivity & Management Review,* 20: 4: 397–404.

Perry, J. L. 1982. "Measuring Public Service Motivation: An Assessment of Construct Reliability and Validity." *Journal of Public Administration Research and Theory,* 6: 1: 5–22.

Perry J. L. and L. R. Wise 1990. "The Motivational Bases of Public Service." *Public Administration Review,* 50: 3: 367–73.

Phase 5 Consulting Group Inc. 2005. *Citizens First 4.* Survey. Toronto: Institute for Citizen-Centred Service and Institute for Public Administration of Canada.

Pollitt, C. et al. 2004. *Agencies: how governments do things through semi-autonomous organizations.* New York: Palgrave Macmillan.

Posner, P. 2002. "Accountability challenges of third party government." In *The Tools of Government: A Guide to the New Governance*, ed. L. Salomon. New York: Oxford University Press, chapter 18.

Prottas, J. M. 1979. *People Processing: The Street-Level Bureaucrat in Public Service Bureaucracies*. Lexington, MA: D.C. Heath & Company.

Public Sector Service Delivery Council 2006. "Opportunities for Inter-jurisdictional Service Delivery Collaboration." Prepared for deputy minister's meeting, October 10–11, Montebello, Quebec.

Rawson, B. 1991. "Public Service 2000 Service to the Public Task Force: Findings and Implications." *Canadian Public Administration*, 34: 3: 490–500.

Reed, B. 2004. "Accountability in a Shared Services World." In *Future Challenges for e-Government*, eds. J. Halligan and T. Moore. Canberra: Government of Australia (AGIMO), vol I: 139.

Reid, J. 2004. "Holding Governments Accountable by Strengthening Access to Information Laws and Information Management Practices." In *E-Government Reconsidered: Renewal of Governance for the Knowledge Age*, eds. L. Oliver and L. Sanders. Regina: Canadian Plains Research Center, chapter 5.

Ritz, Adrian 2009. "Public Service Motivation and Organizational Performance in Swiss Federal Government." *International Review of Administrative Sciences*, 75: 1: 53–78.

Roth, V. J., L. Bozinoff and P. MacIntosh 1990. "Public Opinion and the Measurement of Consumer Satisfaction with Government Services." *Canadian Public Administration*, 33: 4: 571–583.

Roy, J. 2003. "The Relational Dynamics of E-Governance: A Case Study of the City of Ottawa." *Public Performance and Management Review*, 26: 4: 391–403.

Roy, J. 2005. "Services, Security, Transparency and Trust: Government Online or Governance Renewal in Canada?" *International Journal of E-Government Research*, 1: 1: 48–58.

Roy, J. 2006a. *E-Government in Canada: Transformation for the Digital Age*. Ottawa: University of Ottawa Press.

Roy, J. 2006b "E-Service Delivery and New Governance Capacities: 'Service Canada' as a Case Study." *International Journal of Services Technology and Management*, 7: 3: 253–272.

Rucci, A. J., S. P. Kirk and R. T. Quinn, 1998 (January–February). "The Employee-Customer-Profit Chain at Sears." *Harvard Business Review*, 83–97.

Ryan, C. and P. Walsh 2004. "Collaboration of public sector agencies: reporting and accountability challenges." *International Journal of Public Sector Management*, 17: 7: 1–26.

Savoie, D. J. 2004. "Searching for accountability in a government without boundaries." *Canadian Public Administration*, 47: 1: 1–26.

Schachter, H. L. 1995. "Reinventing Government or Reinventing Ourselves: Two Models of Improving Government Performance." *Public Administration Review*, 55: 6: 530–537.

Schellong, A. and A. Goethe 2006. *CRM in the Public Sector – Towards a conceptual research framework*. Cambridge, MA: Harvard University, National Center for Digital Government.

Schlesinger L. and J. L. Heskett, 1991a. "The Service-Driven Service Company." *Harvard Business Review*, 69: 5: 71–81.

Schlesinger L. and J. L. Heskett 1991b. "How Does Service Drive the Service Company?" *Harvard Business Review*, 69: 6: 146+.

Schlesinger, L., J. L. Heskett and W. E. Sasser 1997. *The Service Profit Chain*. New York: The Free Press.

Schmidt, F. and T. Strickland 1998a (December). "Client Satisfaction Surveying: Common Measurements Tool." Ottawa: Canadian Centre for Management Development. Available at www.gov.mb.ca/stem/stm/pdfs/CCSN_CMT.pdf.

Schmidt, F. and T. Strickland 1998b (December). "Client Satisfaction Surveying: A Manager's Guide." Ottawa: Canadian Centre for Management Development. Available at www.gov.mb.ca/stem/stm/pdfs/CCSN_guide.pdf.

Scott, J. K. 2006. "'E' the People: Do U.S. Municipal Government Web Sites Support Public Involvement?' *Public Administration Review*, 66: 3: 341–353

Scottish Executive 2006. *Transforming Public Services: The Next Stage of Reform*. Edinburgh: The Scottish Executive. www.scotland.gov.uk/Resource/Doc/130092/0031160.pdf.

Séguin, F. 1991. "Service to the Public: A Major Strategic Change." *Canadian Public Administration*, 34: 3: 465–473.

Seidle, F. L. 1995. *Rethinking the Delivery of Public Services to Citizens*. Montreal: Institute for Research on Public Policy.

Shane, P. 2004. *The Prospects for Political Renewal Through the Internet*. London, UK: Routledge.

Shirky, C. 2008. *Here comes everybody: the power of organizing without organizations*. New York: Penguin.

Skelcher, J. 2005. "Jurisdictional Integrity, Polycentrism, and the Design of Democratic Governance." *Governance*, 18: 1: 89–110.

Skrtic, T. M., W. Sailor and K. Gee 1996. "Voice, Collaboration, and Inclusion: Democratic Themes in Educational and Social Reform Initiatives" *Remedial and Special Education*, 17: 3: 142–157.

Sossin, L. 2002. "Discretion Unbound: Reconciling the Charter and Soft Law." *Canadian Public Administration*, 45: 4: 465–489.

Stewart, J. and P. Kringas 2003. "Change Management: Strategy and Values in Six Agencies from the Australian Public Service." *Public Administration Review*, 63: 6: 675–688.

Stipak, B. 1979. "Citizen Satisfaction with Urban Services: Potential Misuse as a Performance Indicator." *Public Administration Review*, 39: 1: 46–52.

Stoker, G. 2004 "New Localism, Participation, and Networked Community Governance." Paper. Manchester, UK: University of Manchester, Institute for

Political and Economic Governance (IPEG), 19 (table 2). www.ipeg.org.uk/papers/ngcnewloc.pdf.

Stoker, G. 2006. "Public Value Management – A New Narrative for Networked Governance?" *American Review of Public Administration*, 36: 1: 41–57.

Swiss, J. E. 1992. "Adapting Total Quality Management (TQM) to Government." *Public Administration Review*, 52: 4: 356–362.

Tapscott, D. and A. D. Williams 2006. *Wikinomics – How Mass Collaboration Changes Everything*. New York: Penguin Group.

Tapscott, D., A. D. Williams and D. Herman, 2008. *Government 2.0: Transforming Government and Governance for the Twenty-First Century*. Report. Toronto: New Paradigm: The Business Innovation Company. http://newparadigm.inorbital.com.

Taras, D. and A. Tupper 1994. "Politics and deficits: Alberta's challenge to the Canadian political agenda." In *Canada: The State of the Federation 1994*, eds. M. Brown and J. Hiebert. Kingston, ON: Institute of Intergovernmental Relations, chapter 4. www.queensu.ca/iigr/pub/archive/SOTF/SOTF1994.pdf.

Traut, C. A., R. Larsen and S. Feimer 2000. "Hanging On or Fading Out: Job Satisfaction and the Long-Term Worker." *Public Personnel Management*, 29: 4: 343–350.

Treadwell, J. 2007 (May). "Shared Governance and Collaboration." Prepared for *EDUCAUSE Australasia 2007 – Advancing Knowledge Pushing Boundaries*, Melbourne, Australia. www.caudit.edu.au/educauseaustralasia07/authors_papers/jane-treadwell.pdf.

Turner, T. 2004. "Accountability in Cross-Tier E-Government Integration." In *Future Challenges for e-Government: Collective Accountability*, eds. J. Halligan and T. Moore. Canberra: Government of Australia, 128–138.

United Kingdom 2005. Cabinet Office. *Transformational Government: Enabled by Technology*. Norwich, UK: HMSO.

United Kingdom 2006a. Prime Minister's Strategy Unit. *The UK Government's Approach to Public Service Reform*. London. www.strategy.gov.uk/downloads/work_areas/public_service_reform/sj_pamphlet.pdf.

United Kingdom 2006b. Office of Government Commerce. *UK 2006 OGC Gateway Review for Programmes and Projects*. London. www.ogc.gov.uk .

United Kingdom 2007. Aylesbury Vale District Council, Buckinghamshire County Council, Chiltern District Council, South Bucks District Council and Wycombe District Council. *Effective, Strong and Integrated Local Government in Buckinghamshire: A Pioneering, Pathfinder Model for Enhanced Two Tier Working*. Buckinghamshire, UK. https://isa.chiltern.gov.uk/democracy/Data/Cabinet/20080422/Agenda/Agenda%20Enclosure%207.pdf.

United Nations 2008. *From e-Government to Connected Governance*. United Nations e-Government Survey 2008. New York: UN DESA. http://unpan1.un.org/intradoc/groups/public/documents/un/unpan028607.pdf.

Van de Walle, S. et al. 2008. "Trust in the Public Sector: Is there any Evidence for a Long-term Decline?" *International Review of Administrative Sciences*, 74: 1: 47–64.

Van Goor, H. and B. Stuiver 1998. "Can Weighting Compensate for Nonresponse Bias in a Dependent Variable? An Evaluation of Weighing Methods to Correct for Substantive Bias in a Mail Survey among Dutch Municipalities." *Social Science Research*, 27: 481–499.

Van Ryzin, G. G. and S. Immerwahr 2007. "Importance-Performance Analysis of Citizen Satisfaction Surveys." *Public Administration Review*, 85: 1: 215–226.

Van Slyke, D. 2002. "The Public Management Challenges of Contracting with Non-Profits for Social Services." *The International Journal of Public Administration*, 25: 4: 489–517.

Vandenabeele, W. 2009. "The mediating effect of job satisfaction and organizational commitment on self-reported performance: more robust evidence of the PSM-performance relationship." *International Review of Administrative Studies*, 75:1: 11–35.

Vardon, S. 2000. "One-To-One: the Art of Personalised Service." Paper presented at *Case Management: Fact or Fiction,* University of Melbourne, 11 February.

Varney, Sir D. 2006 (December). *Service transformation: A better service for citizens and businesses, a better deal for the taxpayer.* Report (Varney Review). London, UK: The Stationery Office, HM Treasury. www.hm-treasury.gov.uk/d/pbr06_varney_review.pdf.

Venkatachalam, J. 1998. "Literature on Organizational Commitment: A Review." *South Asian Journal of Management*, 22: 3: 18–28.

Watad, M. and S. Ospina 1999. "Integrated Managerial Training: A Program for Strategic Management Development." *Public Personnel Management*, 28: 2: 185–195.

Weedon, C. 1997. *Feminist Practice & Poststructuralist Theory.* New York: Blackwell Publishing.

Whitener, E. M. 2001. "Do High Commitment Human Resource Practices affect Employee Commitment? A cross-level analysis using hierarchical linear modeling." *Journal of Management*, 27: 5: 515–535.

Whitehead M. 2003. "In the Shadow of Hierarchy: Policy Reform and Urban Regeneration in the West Midlands." *Area*, 35: 1: 6–14.

Wilkins, P. 2002. "Accountability and joined-up government." *Australian Journal of Public Administration*, 61: 1: 114–119.

Williams, A. D. 2008 (January). *Government 2.0: Wikinomics and the Challenge to Government.* http://networkedgovernment.ca/cp.asp?pid=67.

Woock, R. R. 1981. "Sociological Analysis and Comparative Education." *International Review of Education*, 27: 4: 411–25.

Woodward, V. 2003. "Participation the community work way." *International Journal of Healthcare Technology and Management*, 5: 1/2: 3–19.

Yankelovich, D. 1999. *The Magic of Dialogue – Transforming Conflict Into Cooperation*. New York: Simon and Schuster.

Yeatman, A. and K. Owler 2001. "The Role of Contract in the Democratisation of Service Delivery." *Law in Context*, 18: 2: 34–56.

Yeatman, A., G. W. Dowsett and D. Gursansky 2009. *Individualization and the Delivery of Welfare Services: Contestation and Complexity*. Basingstoke: Palgrave Macmillan.

Yukon 2008. Public Service Commission. "Yukon Government Employee Engagement Survey: Employee Report." Whitehorse, YU: Yukon Public Service Commission. www.psc.gov.yk.ca/pdf/2008_emp_engagement_report.pdf.

INDEX

involvement in service delivery, 137
involvement in service design, 5, 118–120, 130–131, 138–139
knowledge creation by, 140
priorities of, 138–139
Sierra, 92
silos, 47, 129, 141
Singapore, 113, 136
single-window service
    creation of, 34–35
    impediments to, 50
    limitations to, 106
    move away from, 137, 142, 145
    role of, 47
Six Sigma, 82, 84
social networking, 112, 144
social programs, 47, 110, 126n13
Social Union Framework Agreement (SUFA), 109
Southern Alberta Child and Youth Network, 122
special operating agencies, 14
specialization, 48
staff *See* public servants
stakeholders, 119, 120, 135, 137, 138
stereotypes about government services, 44, 47
surveys
    accuracy of, 38, 42–43
    causality, 39–42, 50, 51n4
    creating knowledge, 37–44
    customer satisfaction, 6
    data analysis, 40
    of employees, 55–56
    epistemological approach, 45
    history of, 33–36
    problems with, 37, 39, 47–48, 149–150
    representativeness of, 37–39, 50
    response rates, 38–39
    review of, 37
    rise of, 31

subjectivity of, 42–44, 50
value of, 31–32, 32–33, 42, 43
Switzerland, 107, 111

T

tax filing, 15–16, 28, 134, 147–148
taxpayers, 21–22, 46–47
technological innovation
    channel options, 136
    early, 152–153
    importance of, 10
    integrative services through, 142
telephone-based service, 34–35, 47, 99, 136
Tellier, Paul, 52
311 contact point, 3, 125
Tlicho Community Services Agency, 127n13
total quality movements, 1–2
traditional public administration, 155–156
training of public servants, 63, 77–81, 83, 124
transactional models, 20
transparency
    in e-government, 134
    in Government 2.0, 131
    in private-sector partnerships, 93, 95, 98
    of quality monitoring, 154
    in shared governance, 98
Treasury Board Secretariat, 34, 79
trust
    among public servants, 7
    in e-government, 134
    effects of service reform, 49
    forms of, 30
    in governments, 2, 16, 18, 23–24, 30, 31, 35, 40, 41
    and horizontal governance, 24
    inter-jurisdictional, 116–117
    measuring, 23–24
    in network governance, 121

Governance Series Publications

27. Ruth Hubbard and Gilles Paquet (eds) 2010
   The Case for Decentralized Federalism
26. Gordon DiGiacomo and Maryantonett Flumian (eds) 2010
   The Case for Centralized Federalism
25. Patrice Dutil, Cosmo Howard, John Langford and Jeffrey Roy 2010
   The Service State: Rhetoric, Reality and Promise
24. Ruth Hubbard and Gilles Paquet 2010
   The Black Hole of Public Administration
23. Michael Small 2009
   The Forgotten Peace–Mediation at Niagara Falls, 1914
22. Gilles Paquet 2009
   Crippling Epistemologies and Governance Failures–A Plea for Experimentalism
21. O. P. Dwivedi, Timothy Mau, and Byron Sheldrick (eds) 2009
   The Evolving Physiology of Government–Canadian Public Administration in Transition
20. Caroline Andrews, Ruth Hubbard, and Jeffrey Roy (eds) 2009
   Gilles Paquet–Homo Hereticus
19. Luc Juillet and Ken Rasmussen 2008
   Defending a Contested Ideal–Merit and the Public Service Commission: 1908–2008
18. Luc Juillet et Ken Rasmussen 2008
   À la défense d'un idéal contesté–le principe de mérite et la CFP, 1908–2008
17. Gilles Paquet 2008
   Deep Cultural Diversity–A Governance Challenge
16. Paul Schafer 2008
   Revolution or Renaissance–Making the Transition from an Economic Age to a Cultural Age
15. Gilles Paquet 2008
   Tableau d'avancement–petite ethnographie interprétative d'un certain Canada français
14. Tom Brzustowski 2008
   The Way Ahead–Meeting Canada's Productivity Challenge
13. Jeffrey Roy 2007
   Business and Government in Canada
12. N. Brown and L. Cardinal (eds) 2007
   Managing Diversity–Practices of Citizenship